geo- |jēō |

comb. form

• of or relating to the earth: *geometric, geographic.*

• from Greek gē "earth."

Oxford English Dictionary, 3rd Ed.

 IN THIS ISSUE

4   EDITORIAL
KAREN M'CLOSKEY + KEITH VANDERSYS

6   DOWN TO EARTH
KAREN M'CLOSKEY + KEITH VANDERSYS

12   GROUND COVER
ROBERT GERARD PIETRUSKO

20   CRITICALITY AS INTERPRETATION,
DECEPTION, DISTORTION?
MATTHEW W. WILSON

26   IN CONVERSATION WITH WILLIAM RANKIN

32   VERTICAL MEDIATION AT STANDING ROCK
LISA PARKS

42   OF PITS AND PADS
JEFFREY S. NESBIT + DAVID SALOMON

50   PLANETARY VOYEURISM
DOUGLAS ROBB + KAREN BAKKER

56   UNCOMMON PLANET: GEOSTORIES OF
THE GLOBAL COMMONS
RANIA GHOSN

64   UNCONVENTIONAL RESOURCES
MATTHEW RANSOM

72   IN CONVERSATION WITH JENNIFER GABRYS

78   WHAT ON EARTH?
LUCY R. LIPPARD

80   MAKING THE ROUGH GROUND PLANE
B.W. HIGMAN

86   RECONSTRUCTING THE DENT DU REQUIN
AISLING O'CARROLL

94   THE ROCKS MUST BE STRANGE
NOAH HERINGMAN

100   IN CONVERSATION WITH JANINE RANDERSON

106   GLIMMER: REFRACTING ROCK
SHANNON MATTERN

IMAGE CREDITS
UPCOMING ISSUES

LA+ GEO
EDITORIAL

GEO–Earth–is a word that simultaneously signifies something vast and elemental. It refers both to the planet on which we live and the soil that sustains us. GEO is the physical and representational bedrock of landscape architecture – the foundation of many disciplines from which we draw our knowledge. Geography, geometry, and geology, in particular, are fundamental to our discipline's intellectual core.

This issue of *LA+ Journal* invited contributors to reflect on the evolving objects, instruments, and institutions of geo-related studies. The essays cover a wide range of territory from rocks to rockets, from museums to maps, and from ground to sky. Authors consider how various media, tools, and methods affect practice, and ask where power is lodged in such practices. As Denis Cosgrove once said, "Geography lays particular claim to the globe." Key concepts such as place, space, territory, and region are central to both geography and landscape architecture. The critiques of cartography and GIS that arose from within geography in the 1980s and '90s exerted an especially strong influence on our discipline. Using the work of J.B. Harley and John Pickles, Matthew W. Wilson revisits this important moment in time. Following on this, we spoke with William Rankin about mapping practices and how new technologies like GPS are radically altering how we understand the nature of territory.

Looking to the Cold War agendas of the US Department of Defense, Robert Gerard Pietrusko describes how aerial photographs provided the basis for botanists to interpret vegetation as proxies for understanding ground conditions suitable for troop movement. Furthermore, photographs of aerial accessible landscapes were themselves used as proxies for the landscapes the military wanted to survey but could not access. However, our ability to apprehend these remote landscapes is still dependent upon the manipulation of specific grounds, as Jeffrey S. Nesbit and David Salomon's comparison of Russian and US satellite launch pad sites demonstrates. Continuing in the realm of satellite technologies, Matthew Ransom examines the tension between grassroots organizations and that of oil and gas industry players, like Halliburton and Cabot, in Pennsylvania. Ransom argues that fracking territories are as much a matter of information access as they are energy resource. On this topic of access, we spoke with Jennifer Gabrys on citizens' use of pollution sensors to gather and interpret data, giving rise to alternative environmental narratives. Similarly, Lisa Parks recounts the importance of activists' use of drone-captured video to document both the protests against the construction of an oil pipeline through tribal lands, as well as the aggressive countermeasures taken by law enforcement to squelch the protests. And, in an interview with Janine Randerson, we learned

about artists who use scientific instruments and data in innovative ways to engage the issue of climate change through aesthetically affective and bodily-engaged works.

Two essays explore the role of geometry in the production of landscapes. The mathematics of points, lines, and surfaces fundamentally shapes how we collect, code, and categorize matter. By reconstructing one of Eugène Viollet-le-Duc's Mont Blanc studies, Aisling O'Carroll explores the use of projective geometry to rationalize geological structures, exposing the sleight of hand used by Voillet-le-Duc to fit nature into his preconception of its form. B.W. Higman continues in this vein by tracing our modern predilections toward flatness–visual, material, and political–and the real-world implications that this flattening has on our landscapes.

Another series of essays explores the relationship among geology, extraction, and colonization in distinct ways. Through illustrated "Geostories," Rania Ghosn imaginatively engages the "global commons" of outer space and oceans – resource-rich areas devoid of jurisdictional control and therefore ripe for exploitation. Through the work of architect William Chambers, Noah Heringman revisits the role of the sublime in 18th-century landscape design, offering parallels to today's Anthropocene discourses about environmental depletion. And Shannon Mattern examines how rocks are collected, examined, and displayed as objects of spectacular brilliance – objects that ultimately reflect back on us by illuminating the histories of oppression and marginalization embedded in their extraction.

Douglas Robb and Karen Bakker caution against the totalizing vantage enabled by satellites and other remote sensing technologies and the voyeuristic tendencies of geographers and designers who find and observe climate catastrophes from afar. Similarly, while recounting a flight across the United States, Lucy R. Lippard reflects on the gap between our experiences on the ground and those revealed from an aerial vantage. Can new climate narratives arise from a fusion between these viewpoints, she asks, and might landscape architects be the ones to help with this mediation? With this question in mind, we begin the journal with our own reflections on the tools that have recently become available to landscape architects, followed by the rich and diverse viewpoints on other matters of media. Whether digging deep or flying high, our technologies of sensing, imaging, and extraction further entrench us into the GEO we have made and that continues to make us.

Karen M'Closkey + Keith VanDerSys
Issue Editors

KAREN M'CLOSKEY + KEITH VANDERSYS

DOWN TO EARTH

Karen M'Closkey + Keith VanDerSys are founding partners of PEG office of landscape + architecture and faculty in the Department of Landscape Architecture at the University of Pennsylvania, Stuart Weitzman School of Design. Their recent work explores advances in environmental modeling and simulation tools. They are guest editors of *LA+ Simulation* (2016) and authors of *Dynamic Patterns: Visualizing Landscapes in a Digital Age* (2017).

+ TECHNOLOGY, SPATIAL ANALYTICS, AESTHETICS

In 1957, Sputnik 1 was launched into orbit. On that day, according to media theorist Marshall McLuhan, "Nature ended and Ecology was born," by which he meant that there was no longer any "outside" for the natural world, only an inside of which humans were a part.[1] All did not share this optimistic interpretation of events. Philosopher Hannah Arendt was alarmed at the increasing distance between scientists and the objects of their study, made possible through a "veritable avalanche of fabulous instruments and ever more ingenious machinery."[2] Given the ability of computers to accomplish what the human brain alone could not, Arendt feared that "man can do... what he cannot comprehend."[3] For Arendt, space travel epitomized the quest for the Archimedean point – a supposedly objective position outside of Earth by which we could look down upon ourselves. From this vantage, Arendt argued, we risk reducing humans to nothing more than subjects with "overt behavior."[4] Just over a decade later, the first photograph of Earth from outer space–*Earthrise*–was captured by astronauts aboard Apollo 8. This view was, for some, evidence of our planet's extraordinariness. It encapsulated the sense of an organic and interconnected whole Earth – a planet without borders, a planet that was more atmosphere than solid ground. For the astronauts, ecologists, and environmentalists, "*Earthrise* and its kin...turned the globe back into Earth."[5]

If satellites enabled an all-encompassing image of the Earth, then molecular sensor technologies provided a more localized view. James Lovelock, scientist and originator of the "Gaia hypothesis," developed the Electron Capture Detector (ECD) the same year Sputnik 1 was launched. This device was instrumental to the rise of the environmental movement of the 1960s and early '70s. The information gleaned via ECDs revealed the deleterious effects of the widespread use of synthetic chemicals, providing irrefutable evidence for Rachel Carson's seminal book, *Silent Spring* (1962).[6] Later, data collected with ECDs showed the presence of chlorofluorocarbons in the atmosphere, a discovery that led to research on ozone depletion and the eventual verification of the ozone hole through samples collected with NASA's Nimbus satellite program.[7] Thus, post-war environmentalism grew out of the combination of localized environmental sensing and global environmental change; these tools are what gave rise to the environmentalism that we take for granted today.

The environmental narratives that arose with the development of sensing and sensor instruments–from satellites to ECDs–can be seen to support McLuhan's claim that every new technology creates a new environment.[8] For both material and conceptual reasons, for better and for worse, it was an environment where the distinctions between local and remote, visible and invisible, and inside and outside began to dissolve.

A growing body of literature has continued to revisit the tension between the environmentalism of the Space Age era, and the often-imperialistic rhetoric of "one home, one people" that accompanies its overarching narrative. While some saw the Apollo space photographs as helping galvanize concern about our planet, and the people living on it, others have continued to argue along the lines of Arendt. For example, geographer Denis Cosgrove argues that these images exemplify "the Apollonian urge to establish a transcendental, univocal, and universally valid vantage point from which to sketch a totalizing discourse."[9] More recently, Benjamin Lazier has asked if the whole Earth is simply "a globe in disguise" and that the term "global environment" is "a Frankenstein phrase that sutures together words referring to horizons of incompatible scale and experience. Environments surround us. We live within them. Globes stand before us."[10] Others have also made this distinction between globe and environment. Tim Ingold describes the globe as a view from afar, a lifeless solid, and a "surface waiting to be occupied."[11] He contrasts this to the sphere as an ancient symbol of the lifeworld: "[T]he movement from spherical to global imagery…is a movement from revelation to control, and from partial knowledge to calculated risk," and with this view comes the assumption that the planet is ours to manage.[12] Similarly, Gayatri Chakravorty Spivak writes that "The globe is on our computers. No one lives there. It allows us to think that we can aim to control it."[13] In a later essay, "Earth, Sky, Wind, and Weather," Ingold urges us to leave behind any clear distinction between Earth and sky because such a distinction presumes a horizon and sees Earth as *a surface* upon which things occur. He instead posits that we attend to the "weather-world," which is an "open world" where "there are no insides and outsides," where inhabitants are "immersed in the fluxes of the medium" and "nothing ever stands still."[14] This lived weather-world is, for Ingold, distinct from instrumental observation and lifeless globes.

All of these critiques are concerned about the potentially distancing effects of global views, whether those views are actual photos that see Earth *as object* from afar or, more generally, refer to the disengaging effects of certain technologies. Of course, such views existed (as drawings) long before the development of satellites and computers. The desire to know what we cannot directly see, or to transcend earthly limits and look back upon ourselves, is a pursuit that long predates our ability to do so; although, such images were then limited to the human imagination alone. Once the notion of a global environment came into actual view, the question for many was how to come back down to Earth.

In landscape architecture and the environmental writing that influenced the field, particularly in the USA, the post-Earth Day response was framed in terms drawn from an "ethic of proximity."[15] As Elizabeth Meyer has stated, "[I]f the phenomenology of landscape architecture taps into the concrete experience of a place by its citizens and if those experiences intermingle cyclical natural processes with the rhythms of collective social life, then this type of built work can *redefine what it means to be part of the environment.*"[16] She continues, quoting philosopher Arnold Berleant, that "To grasp environment, every vestige of dualism must be discarded. There is no inside and outside, human being and external world…no discrete self and separate other."[17] In this framework, not only is environment a milieu that is directly experienced, but these experiences are thought to move us to act on behalf of the environment. Empathy is presumed to arise from situated knowledge–a sensing body in a place–rather than more abstract or distanced forms of knowledge acquisition.[18] The sentiment that we pay attention to the dynamics of our environment, and that medium (wind/weather) and substance (ground) are intermingled, is of great significance; however, we do not have to do away with technological mediation altogether in order to achieve this understanding. To the contrary, new tools may at times help us see past the entrenchment of our old tools, providing other ways of defining *what it means to be part of the environment* – ways that do not uphold a binary between global systems of knowledge and localized experience.

There is untapped potential for landscape architects to explore the kinds of tools, such as sensors and remote sensing, that gave rise to the environmentalism of the post-Earth Day era; however, these explorations are still nascent.[19] It is not that digital tools are not employed in landscape architecture–they are indeed prevalent–but that they are used primarily as extensions of methods that can be achieved manually or have been well-established for decades, such as GIS.[20] Perhaps this reticence to explore new tools is due to a belief that, as outlined above, direct and immersive experience is the best way to understand a place *in process*. Yet this distinction between abstract knowledge and embodied experience is not so simple. As Ursula Heise explains, those who privilege a sense of place ethic ignore that "it is not just that local places have changed through increased connectivity but also the structures of perception, cognition, and social expectation associated with them."[21] In other words, we cannot simply "unknow" the perceptions gleaned through our instruments. This is in no way to suggest that there is a replacement for experience–studying the mathematics of waves does not enable one to sail a boat–but rather to argue, as Kathryn Yusoff does, that Ingold's "dialectic of an inside and outside in global thinking no longer has the same purchase when we think about digital earth in which both inside and outside are simultaneously built through the architecture of data."[22] Experience is always already mediated.

Certainly, global views–and any technology, drawing, or policy that makes such outlooks possible–can be used to erase differences and homogenize bodies, rendering the inequities among us invisible.[23] However, the lack of exploration of sensing and computation in landscape architecture has generally not been argued with respect to these concerns; rather, the lack of exploration is due to a persistent divide between physical material and digital media. Yet all media used by landscape architects, including pencil and paper, are intermediaries between the physical world and our perception of it. It is incongruous that, when it comes to design methods that pertain to natural materials and processes, landscape architects have adopted the knowledge provided to us by others who use computation for understanding processes (namely scientists and engineers) without considering how they might change the practices of our own discipline. Rather than assume that the virtual form is immaterial we should instead, as Yusoff argues, "become more precisely attuned to its forms of materiality."[24]

Jennifer Gabrys (interviewed in this issue) has argued that the "one-world" view created by global observation technologies is potentially superseded, or at least disrupted, by the "many-worlds" enabled through in-field, distributed environmental sensors. In her book, *Program Earth*, Gabrys does not consider sensing in terms of a human subject that is "rendered through theories of phenomenological or prosthetic engagement" or where environmental sensors provide "new registers of information for established subjects" but rather, similar to Heise, reflects on how sensing changes the relationships and connections through which subjects act.[25] Thus, for Gabrys, sensing is a process of participation where programmability refers not only to hardware and software but also to the events, experiences, or environments that arise out of sensing practices: "the world of sensors is one of amplified connections."[26] Just as the global environment became political once it was made visible (as action to ban CFCs to "heal" the Ozone Hole demonstrates), so too has citizen sensing which, as Gabrys's work has shown, can lead to action at local levels of government as individuals and communities form constituencies around particular environmental issues, especially pollution.[27] Thus, the difference between the early days of sensing and now is not only in the sheer number of sensing devices but in who is doing the fieldwork.

Optical equipment such as lidar, hyperspectral, multispectral, and thermal imaging, along with machine-learning algorithms, can open up perspectives that aren't solely based on the optics of the human eye. These sensing methods, which are now widely available to landscape architects, might reveal different spatial patterns and material distributions than what our conventional tools allow us to see, and help dislodge some stubborn and problematic divisions. Perhaps one of the most important of these material classifications to challenge—one that is pervasive and has wide-ranging consequences—is the distinction between land and water, which is reinforced through extant data collection and classification practices. Without understanding the biases in the given datasets, we lack the ability to change the practices and resulting maps

1 Marshall McLuhan, "At the moment of Sputnik the planet becomes a global theater in which there are no spectators but only actors," *Journal of Communication* 24, no 1 (March 1974): 49.

2 Hannah Arendt, "The Conquest of Space and the Stature of Man [1963]," *The New Atlantis* (Fall 2007), https://www.thenewatlantis.com/publications/the-conquest-of-space-and-the-stature-of-man.

3 Ibid., 46.

4 Ibid., 54.

5 Benjamin Lazier, "Earthrise; or, The Globalization of the World Picture," *American Historical Review* 116, no 3 (June 2011): 623.

6 Though Carson does not cite Lovelock in her book, the use of ECDs quickly became prevalent and would have been used for much of the research cited in her book. On this history, see Anthony S. Travis, "Detecting Chlorinated Hydrocarbon Residues: Rachel Carson's Villains," *AMBIX* 59, no. 2 (July 2012): 109–30.

7 Sherwood Rowland's Nobel Prize-winning research on ozone depletion (with Mario Molina and Paul Crutzen) was initiated after hearing a talk by James Lovelock in 1972 on CFC detection using the ECD. See "Ozone prophets reach rarefied heights," *NewScientist* (October 21, 1995), https://www.newscientist.com/article/mg14820001-100-ozone-prophets-reach-rarefied-heights/ (accessed January 18, 2020).

8 Marshall McLuhan, "The Invisible Environment: The Future of an Erosion," *Perspecta* 11 (1967): 164.

9 Denis Cosgrove, "Contested Global Visions: One-World, Whole-Earth, and the Apollo Space Photographs," *Annals of the Association of American Geographers* 84, no. 2 (1994): 288.

10 Lazier, "Earthrise; or, The Globalization of the World Picture," 626, 614.

11 Tim Ingold, "Globes and Spheres: The Topology of Environmentalism," in Ingold, *The Perception of the Environment: Essays on Livelihood, Dwelling and Skill* (Routledge, 2000), 214. Though Ingold is referring to the globes found in classrooms rather than Apollo images, the point about a distanced and all-encompassing view applies.

12 Ibid., 216.

13 Gayatri Chakravorty Spivak, *Death of a Discipline* (Columbia University Press, 2003), 72.

14 Tim Ingold, "Earth, Sky, Wind, and Weather," *The Journal of the Royal Anthropological Institute* 13 (2007): S31, S34.

15 Ursula Heise uses this phrase, borrowed from other philosophers, to describe environmentalist perspectives that equate physical closeness to ethical behavior, similar to what is argued by Meyer (see notes 16, 17 below). Ursula K. Heise, *Sense of Place and Sense of Planet: The Environmental Imagination of the Global* (Oxford University Press, 2008), 33.

16 Elizabeth K. Meyer, "The Post-Earth Day Conundrum: Translating Environmental Values into Landscape Design," in Michel Conan (ed.), *Environmentalism in Landscape Architecture* (Dumbarton Oaks, 2000), 243. Italics are ours.

17 Ibid., 193.

18 Heise, 30.

19 There is a small but growing group of landscape architects exploring remote sensing, such as the Dredge Research Collaborative, Bradley Cantrell, Chistophe Girot, and Karl Kullmann, among others.

and models that reinforce static and bounded readings of landscapes. While the Earth is pervasively sensed, rarely is the publicly available data appropriate for localized applications – data is either outdated or too coarse to capture the subtle, yet consequential, modulations that are the drivers and registers of environmental changes. Expanding our sensory practices opens up additional ways of seeing and might enable us to better engage the dynamic material conditions characteristic of the many places where we work.

One example to highlight our point is to consider the use of multispectral imaging to survey wetlands and coasts. As dunes and marshes migrate upland, which is occurring faster than at any point in recorded history, the need for littoral adaptation increases. Frequent alterations in tides, salinity, and sediment make such habitats difficult to document (whether using field surveying or traditional aerial photography). In this situation, multispectral cameras hold promise. Both organic and inorganic materials have unique spectral signatures from reflected or absorbed electromagnetic waves.[28] Though satellite-captured images can gather multispectral data, the resolution is too low to see the subtle topographic variation on which wetland grasses depend. By contrast, a small drone fitted with a multispectral camera can produce high-resolution imagery of plant species and their distribution (as seen in the image below). A comparison of these image sets enables the detection of changes related to environmental stressors in wetland plant communities well before such changes are visible to the naked eye. This information can be used to help determine actions, for example, where to add or reduce sediment to maintain critical habitats. Not only that, once a design intervention is made, the effect can then be monitored and the design adjusted accordingly. Surely multispectral imaging has its own limitations but it is one tool within a digital toolkit that uses geolocation and in-field plant sampling as a basis for imaging and modeling, linking across scales and collapsing any meaningful distinction between local observation and whole Earth technologies.

In the above examples, whether pollution sensing or wetland monitoring, data are collected locally by people sensing *in place*; however, the physical world fashioned as such will not assuage those who are concerned that nature and environment are evened out in a digital space of ones and zeros. In the abstraction of a computational environment, what is not sensed and coded does not exist. Like the critiques of globes outlined earlier, or the reduction of life to overt behavior of which Arendt warned, architect John May cautions about the rise of the *managerial surface*—a statistical-electrical control space—where data collection has "reoriented and restructured the entire scientific-bureaucratic apparatus that today takes 'the environment' as its object of concern."[29] According to May, this world of pervasive sensing simply extends the project of modernity while simultaneously claiming to help with the cleanup of its worst offenses. The control and operation of the managerial surface is "made to dream in the language of solutions while remaining wide-awake to the historical absurdity of that very discourse."[30] Perhaps not surprisingly, he uses the embedded sensor network at Freshkills, a 2,200-acre park-capped landfill, as emblematic of this incongruity.

We share these concerns. Today, images of the global environment abound: atmospheric carbon simulations, online sea-level rise maps, nighttime views from space—constructed with thousands of images rather than a single photograph like *Earthrise*—showing a glimmering planet and *presumed* areas of urbanization. Each one can reinforce narratives that are used to structure actions by the powerful few in the name of many;

however, if one agrees that every new technology creates a new environment, then environmental sensing and modeling tools can also be used to structure different points of view, as several of the essays and interviews in this issue of *LA+* demonstrate.

We do not have to zealously embrace new technologies to know that the media described by McLuhan are as much "our" environment as the medium described by Ingold and others, making distinctions such as embodied and abstract, the near and far, the unmediated and the mediated, not particularly helpful or even tenable. We are not claiming that we should use these tools for the sake of innovation or efficiency, but rather as a means to question the given data sets and cartographic practices of our own discipline, and to develop literacy in the means and methods that underpin and authorize the status quo of material and land use classifications. Exploring an expanded set of tools and methods to bring the changing nature of environmental patterns down to earth and into view is something landscape architects can do. It is through the specificity of localized topography, vegetation, animals, and people in particular places that these environmental changes even matter.

20 On the difference between using computers as extensions of well-established methods versus using computation for the development of different methods, see Karen M'Closkey, "Structuring Relations: From Montage to Model in Composite Imaging," in Charles Waldheim & Andrea Hansen (eds) *Composite Landscapes: Photomontage and Landscape Architecture* (Hatje Cantz and Isabella Stewart Gardner Museum, 2015), 116–31.

21 Heise, *Sense of Place and Sense of Planet*, 54.

22 Kathryn Yusoff, "Excess, Catastrophe, and Climate Change," *Environment and Planning D: Society and Space* 27 (2009): 1018.

23 One example of a globalizing/homogenizing view that can render inequality invisible is some of the discourse about the "Anthropocene." For critiques of the Anthropocene, see the work of TJ Demos, Donna Haraway, and Jason W. Moore, among many others.

24 Kathryn Yusoff, "Excess, Catastrophe, and Climate Change," 1018.

25 Jennifer Gabrys, *Program Earth: Environmental Sensing Technology and the Making of a Computational Planet* (University of Minnesota Press, 2016), 22.

26 This quote is the opening sentence in Jennifer Gabrys, *How to Do Things with Sensors* (University of Minnesota Press, 2019), 1.

27 Helen Pritchard & Jennifer Gabrys, "From Citizen Sensing to Collective Monitoring: Working through the Perceptive and Affective Problematics of Environmental Pollution," *GeoHumanities* 2, no. 2 (2016): 354–71.

28 While individual species have tight spectral ranges, a trustworthy spectral database requires multiple collection records to best capture what that range is, given that leafing, tidal stage, and seasonality all effect reflectance values.

29 John May, "Logic of the Managerial Surface," *PRAXIS: Journal of Writing + Building* 13 (2011): 117. Also on data fetishism see much work by Shannon Mattern. Of particular relevance to this essay is "Methodolatry and the Art of Measure," *Places* (November 2013), https://placesjournal.org/article/methodolatry-and-the-art-of-measure/ and "Mapping's Intelligent Agents," *Places* (September 2017), https://placesjournal.org/article/mappings-intelligent-agents/.

30 May, ibid., 121.

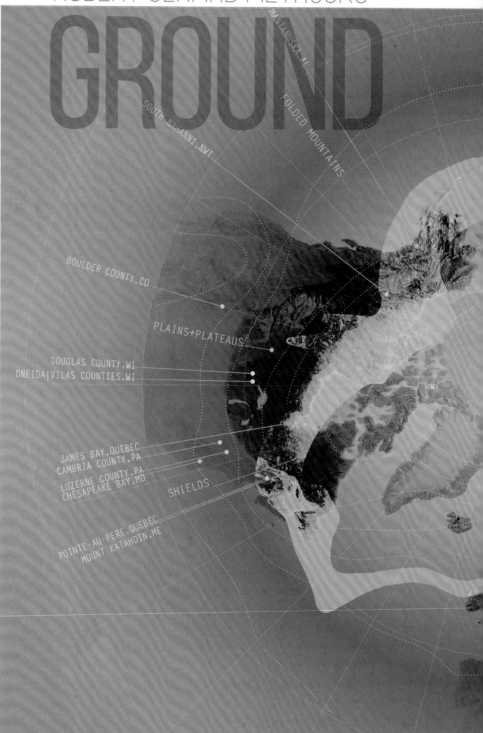

ROBERT GERARD PIETRUSKO

GROUND

MATANUSKA.AK

SOUTH NAHANNI.NWT

FOLDED MOUNTAINS

BOULDER COUNTY.CO

PLAINS+PLATEAUS

DOUGLAS COUNTY.WI
ONEIDA|VILAS COUNTIES.WI

90W

JAMES BAY.QUEBEC
CAMBRIA COUNTY.PA

LUZERNE COUNTY.PA
CHESAPEAKE BAY.MD

SHIELDS

POINTE-AU-PERE.QUEBEC
MOUNT KATAHDIN.ME

0   1000

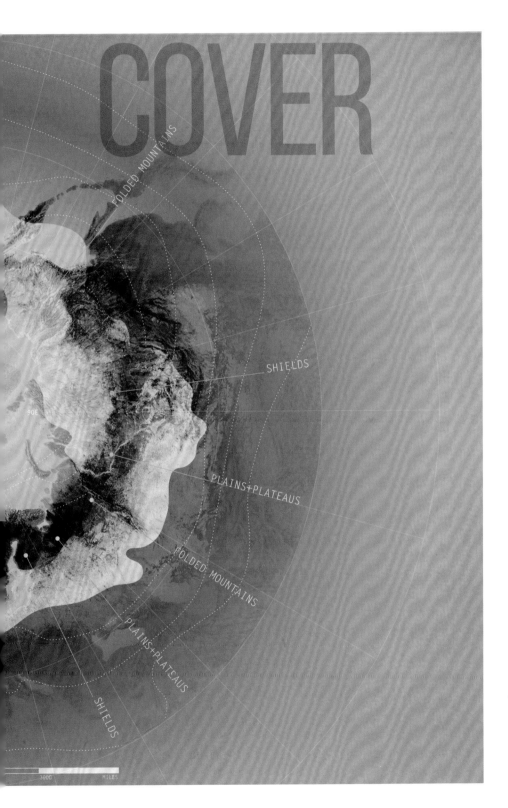

COVER

Robert Gerard Pietrusko is a designer living in Somerville, Massachusetts. His research focuses on geographic representation and the history of spatial data sets. His design work is part of the permanent collection of the Fondation Cartier in Paris and has been exhibited in over 15 countries at venues such as MoMA, ZKM Center for Art & Media, and the Venice Architecture Biennale, among others. Pietrusko is currently an associate professor of landscape architecture at Harvard University's Graduate School of Design.

✛ GEOSCIENCE, MILITARY SCIENCES, BOTANY

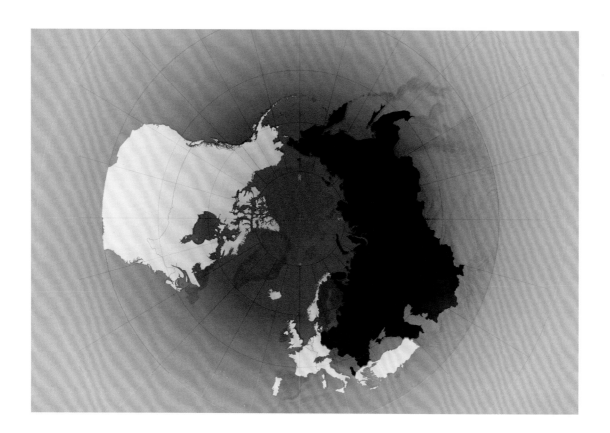

In the first decade of the Cold War, a new geopolitical epistemology emerged for US military strategists. Without direct access to Communist political intentions or to the vast interiors of the Sino-Soviet Bloc, these strategists were forced to derive intelligence through indirect means – by inference, by proxy, and by surrogacy. Military cartographers who formerly depended on direct surveying to create topographic maps now had to adapt to these inaccessible "denied territories."[1] By enlisting botanists and ecologists, they developed techniques of vegetal analysis through which they could indirectly map the Soviet landscape.

The geopolitical context of this research altered how botanists understood the matter of their fieldwork and how analysts and cartographers interpreted aerial reconnaissance photography. As a result, a new concept–photobotany–emerged. For both military analysts and botanists who worked "photobotanically," vegetation was an intensely studied subject but ironically disappeared as a thing in and of itself. Instead, vegetation became a new form of photographic media through which strategic territorial knowledge flowed.

New Proximities

Immediately following the Second World War, US strategists began using new map projections to highlight spatial relationships between the capitalist West and communist East. The shortest distance between the Cold War superpowers was not across the Atlantic Ocean, as conventional maps might show, but over the North Pole. Map projections like the Polar Stereographic highlighted this relationship. The creation of these maps was informed by advances in aviation that increased the range of aerial bombers and, from 1949, by the presence of nuclear arsenals held by both the USA and the USSR. As military strategists considered the flight paths of bomber planes carrying nuclear payloads to densely populated targets, these projections shook them out of what John Holmes called "our Mercatorian vision" and highlighted the true strategic geography of the Cold War.[2] By tracing the radius-of-action of a B-52 bomber onto a polar-projected map, military cartographers produced a new and intense proximity between East and West.

These maps highlighted other types of proximity as well. The Old and New Worlds weren't only physically adjacent in absolute space, they were also adjacent in the abstract, multi-dimensional space of shared ecological characteristics – a space that was indifferent to geopolitical boundaries. Within the polar map projections, northern lands surrounding the Arctic clearly exhibited similar geologic formations (notably, folded mountains, shields, and plateaus); within the northern latitudes there were similar climatic conditions in both the Eastern and Western hemispheres; and, with respect to vegetation, similar species could be found distributed throughout the northern territories. Acknowledging these shared features was not merely encyclopedic, they collectively gave a common definition to a vast arctic and subarctic area. According to Canadian geologist Moira Dunbar, writing in 1966, "It is, in fact, the vegetation, along with the climate, that forms the chief unifying factor that makes it possible to speak of [this territory] as one region in spite of all the variety of topography."[3]

Though these similarities had been known to natural scientists for a long time, in the context of the early Cold War, they took on a new geopolitical importance. The US Department of Defense believed that detailed information about these natural features was strategically significant. But to interpret them, intelligence analysts and cartographers would require disciplinary knowledge outside of their conventional training. As a result, the US military mobilized geological, ecological, and botanical expertise that had not previously been considered militarily useful. In one important example, the Office of Naval Research (ONR) contracted three plant ecologists–Hugh T. O'Neill, Arthème Dutilly, and Herbert C. Hanson–for a series of classified research projects in the subarctic region of North America.[4] All three were faculty at the Catholic University of America, where O'Neill and Dutilly were also co-directors of the University's newly formed Arctic Institute, and heads of the Langlois Herbarium – one of the largest in the US at the time.[5] Their ecological knowledge didn't only offer new reconnaissance techniques, it also offered a plausible cover story. By contracting natural scientists in this capacity, the military could obscure research that might otherwise be seen as anticipatory of an armed conflict between the USA and the USSR. As one journalist reported about O'Neill's expeditions, "He went to Alaska recently with the army quartermaster corps apparently to study the breeding places of Alaska's 'sabre-toothed mosquitoes.' Officials of the corps indicate, however, that his work is of a 'top secret' nature and involves something highly important to the armed forces."[6] In a state of associations that might surprise contemporary sensibilities, conventionally trained academic botanists and ecologists were working on classified research in close collaboration with the Department of Defense, the CIA, and Naval Intelligence. These contracts

resulted in a new exchange of information between disciplines that profoundly affected both.

Between 1948 and 1953, O'Neill and his colleagues developed botanical techniques for the ONR that were seen as having tactical military significance. First, they demonstrated that individual vegetal species could indicate underlying ground conditions that affected the mobility of troops and artillery. Furthermore, this vegetation could be interpreted from aerial photographs and thus alleviated the need to map the ground directly. The Navy saw this as especially useful in future wartime scenarios with the Soviet Union where cartographers would not have access to enemy-held ground. Secondly, O'Neill and his colleagues speculated that through these same small-scale ecological relationships they could model one region of the world for another – namely, that the subarctic vegetation of North America could act as a surrogate for vast expanses of the Soviet Union, China, and communist satellite countries. This second aspect of their work transcended the mere mingling of 20th-century botanical methods with military tactics into the realm of global geopolitics.

Scale One: Tactical Vegetation

The research conducted by O'Neill and his colleagues was a reinterpretation of botanical methods within the context of military intelligence. The relationship between vegetation and its environmental setting–namely soil–had long been a research topic for botanists. In O'Neill's work, however, this relationship was reframed in terms of military tactics, where the correspondence between different vegetation and their underlying ground conditions was treated as a proxy for troop mobility. He highlighted the importance of terrain intelligence within military strategy and the mediating role that vegetation could play in decoding terrain's operational capacities and constraints. Writing in 1953, O'Neill attempted a brief but revealing theory of "tactical" vegetation. One of the several ways that he claimed vegetation could be understood tactically was its indexical capacity for troop mobility. "Vegetation," he wrote, "may *indicate* roughly the extent to which the soil and/or subsoil underneath it, retard or accelerate movement – this last point is the principal object of this study."[7] As a result, O'Neill and his colleagues analyzed vegetation not on its own terms, but as an indicator of slope, soil type, and soil moisture – all characteristics of the ground which were crucial for the movement of troops and artillery.

The ONR funded numerous expeditions in the subarctic region of North America for O'Neill, Dutilly,

Hanson, and their PhD students, where they used conventional ecological field methods for the purpose of terrain analysis. On a 1952 expedition to Canada's South Nahanni Mountains, they studied scrub birch, willow, and alder trees. Here, they reported that, "[b]irch-covered slopes with bushes not taller than waist-high afford the best and driest means of ascending slopes" whereas "slopes covered with willows and alders are the wettest and worst routes of ascent and descent." Though their research methods were botanical, their findings clearly communicated the priority given to military concerns. In a different research setting, O'Neill may have treated alders to a more neutral description; however, in these reports they were repeatedly described as a treacherous indicator when viewed with the mindset of military mobility.

Sites with different vegetation, and different soil, resulted in different forms of tactical information. On an expedition in August 1952, Dutilly traveled to the James Bay region of Quebec to conduct fieldwork along the Albany River. Here, he studied the relationship between black spruce trees, the level of the water table, and the possibility for movement, noting unexpectedly that "the slope of the terrain is relatively unimportant, while the height of the water table is by far the most important factor influencing travel conditions...A difference of a few inches...causes a profound difference in the vegetation...an extremely sensitive indicator of the water table." This fieldwork directly informed how military strategists interpreted the landscape. With an earlier vegetal sensibility, an analyst might have understood black spruce along the Albany River as an opportunity for camouflage, cover, and concealment. This species was now read differently. It indicated the landscape's slope, soil type, and wetness – in short, its capacity for military movements. With this knowledge, the ground could be mapped accordingly.

To readers acquainted with 20th-century ecological theories, the methods deployed by O'Neill and his colleagues will sound familiar. They were an application of the "plant indicator" concept developed by famed ecologists Fredric Clements, John Weaver, and others, during the 1920s and 1930s.[8] As part of his theory of vegetal climax, Clements studied how plants and plant communities located themselves in response to nuanced environmental conditions and thus "indicated" these conditions. Though these techniques were part of an ecologist's disciplinary knowledge at the time—and would therefore be known to ecologists and botanists alike—there was a more explicit lineage. Herbert Hanson studied with both Clements and Weaver at the University of Kansas. He accompanied Clements during several of the famous field studies and his doctoral dissertation was advised by Weaver.[9] As a result, Hanson and O'Neill directly cited Clements and Weaver in their work despite writing within the context of classified military reports where academic citations were rarely found.

By acknowledging their use of the plant indicator concept, there is something unexpected about the findings of O'Neill, Hanson, and their colleagues – namely, what these botanists stated that plants now indicated. In their analysis, plants were not merely indicators for ground or soil conditions in descriptive naturalistic terms. Instead, plants directly indexed the ground's capacity to support military activities. The point is subtle but important. ONR did not enlist botanists to conduct botanical research that resulted in standard botanical findings to be interpreted later by analysts for their military significance. Instead, O'Neill and his team translated vegetation *directly* into tactical terms. In this process, they modified botanical methods into techniques of reconnaissance. Vegetation became a channel through which knowledge of the terrain and potential military mobility flowed – vegetal species themselves were no longer the object of botanical inquiry.

Scale Two: Photo-determined Communities

Within this new context, the use of aerial photography was another significant difference between O'Neill's approach and standard ecological methods of the time. Concurrent

1 Donald Rumsfeld, "Message of Secretary of Defense Donald H. Rumsfeld To the Veterans of Cold War Overflights of 'Denied Territories' On the Occasion of The Early Cold War Overflights Symposium," in R. Cargill Hall & Clayton D. Laurie [eds], *Early Cold War Overflights, 1950–1956: Symposium Proceedings* [Office of the Historian, National Reconnaissance Office, 2003].

2 John Holmes, "Foreword," in R. St.J. MacDonald [ed.], *The Arctic Frontier* [University of Toronto Press, 1966], i.

3 Moira Dunbar, "The Arctic Setting," in *The Arctic Frontier*, ibid., 15.

4 Hugh O'Neill, *Investigation of Methods for Determining Terrain Conditions by Interpretation of Vegetation from Aerial Photography, Part 1: General Principles of Interpretation of Vegetation and their Incorporation into Keys* [Defense Technical Information Center, 1953]; O'Neill, ibid., Part 2: *Interpretation of Vegetation on Aerial Photographs of the Chesapeake Bay, A Type Of Inland Shores*; O'Neill, ibid., *Part 3: Interpretation of Vegetation on Aerial Photographs of the Arctic and Subarctic Regions* [Arctic Institute, Catholic University of America, 1953].

5 Bernard Boivin, "Ernest Lepage and Arthème Dutilly, their Travels and Herbaria," *Taxon* 32, no. 1 (February 1983): 94.

6 Anon, "Famed Scientist Priest Won Fight Against Polio," *The Register* 23, no. 50 [Denver: December 14, 1947], 4. I have found no other evidence that Dr. O'Neill ever researched or published work on "sabre-toothed mosquitoes," perhaps substantiating the anonymous journalist's insinuation that this was a cover story.

7 O'Neill, *Investigation of Methods: Part 1*, 4.3.

8 Frederic E. Clements, *Plant Indicators: The Relation of Plant Communities to Process and Practice* [The Carnegie Institution, 1920]; Frederic E. Clements, *Plant Succession and Indicators* [The Carnegie Institution, 1928]; Frederic E. Clements & John E. Weaver, *Plant Ecology*, 2nd Edition [McGraw-Hill Book Company, 1938]; H.L. Shantz, "Plants as Soil Indicators" in *Soils and Men: USDA 1938 Yearbook* [United States Department of Agriculture, 1938].

9 ESA Historical Records Committee, "Herbert C. Hanson," *The Ecological Society of America's History and Records*, https://esa.org/history/hanson-h-c/ [accessed August 11, 2019].

10 Herbert C. Hanson, "Characteristics of Some Grassland, Marsh, and Other Plant Communities in Western Alaska," *Ecological Monographs* 21, no. 4 [October 1951]: 317–78.

Title Page: North American surrogate test sites.

Previous: Cold War polar projection.

Opposite: Nahanni Valley 1952 expedition.

with their expeditions were equally important studies of how vegetation was depicted in high-altitude military photographs. Despite the drastically different materials and vantage points used by fieldwork on the one hand, and aerial photography on the other, these two research methods were profoundly entangled in O'Neill's project. As a result, aerial photography affected how the botanists conducted their work in two fundamental ways: first, it altered how they defined the plant communities that they studied; and second, it shaped the language that they used to describe these species.

Their altered definition of a plant community was subtle but radical. O'Neill's team studied and classified only vegetation that could be perceived in a photograph shot from a particular altitude – that of an Air Force reconnaissance plane. As a result, plant species that were small, sparse, or thrived in the shadows of other vegetation were not studied.[10] Even species that might be good indicators of ground conditions were not considered if they could not produce the proper spatial extent in these photographs. With an understanding of how plant communities are defined relative to their larger ecoregion, it could be argued that O'Neill included aerial photographs—and their remote interpreters—within his definition of the ecoregion and allowed

these technical processes to determine what species were included in the community.

For the species that were part of this photo-determined community, O'Neill and his team researched the photographic tones and textures that they produced and how these were perceived by photo interpreters. Their concern for vegetation's photographic signature affected the language that they used to describe the species. For example, in Dutilly's James Bay study area, black spruce was presented in a panchromatic language: "narrow strips of white or light gray," followed immediately by the military implications of this tonal pattern: "by far, the most feasible overland routes."[11] In the Nahanni Valley, willows were described in a similar way: "gray-toned areas" adjacent to rivers. But in this case, the reader was cautioned that the gray-tones (willows) indicated ground that was difficult to traverse; it was best to follow "dark-toned areas" (white spruce).[12] For botanists who were trained to analyze and describe the minute physical structure of plant species in great detail, the change of language is striking – plant morphology was replaced by photo morphology.[13]

Scale Three: Geographic Surrogates

O'Neill's use of vegetation as a proxy for mobility retooled common botanical techniques for military

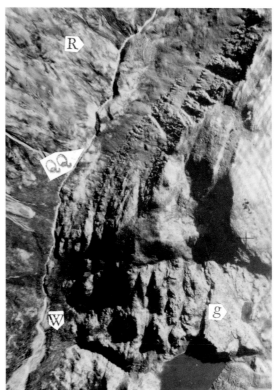

purposes. But through his analysis, vegetation was also a proxy for a radically different scale of reconnaissance and the use of these methods in conjunction with aerial photography emphasized the context in which this knowledge would be used. O'Neill and his colleagues reasoned that photographs taken over the denied territories of the Sino-Soviet Bloc were useful even if they contained no military targets – they implicitly recorded expansive areas of vegetal cover. If the location where the photos were taken had similar geologic and climatic conditions as locations in North America then O'Neill's vegetal analysis could be applied to these inaccessible locations. As a result, O'Neill and his team conducted expeditions in eighteen sites within the subarctic region of North America. Each site provided different climatic, vegetative, and geological conditions that acted as proxies for the terrain that troops might encounter during a possible ground war within the territory of their Communist adversaries.

O'Neill and Dutilly's writing about their expeditions reinforced the sites' proxy status. For instance, in his report on the James Bay expedition, Dutilly described the region as having "vegetation and topography similar to much larger areas in Poland and the USSR" for which his research would have

application.[14] Likewise, in O'Neill's final report on the Nahanni Valley, he stated that "[t]he parallel is likely to be closest between the vegetation on the mountains of Kamchatka."[15] Though Kamchatka was explicitly mentioned, O'Neill clarified that his analysis applied more broadly to numerous Russian mountain ranges and his report included maps of Russian geology to show all of the locations for which his study applied.[16]

The implications of this research were profound. Through the human-scaled analysis of individual North American vegetal species—and the interpretation of their photographic tone—vast geographic territories of the USSR could be mapped indirectly and from afar.

Conclusion: Photobotany

During a 1953 conference sponsored by the Department of Defense, Page Truesdell, an analyst at the Naval Photographic Interpretation Center [NPIC], made the case for a new method of aerial photographic analysis that he called "photobotany." Appealing to intelligence analysts in the audience and their concerns for finding military targets in the complicated patterns of aerial photographs, he invited them to consider additional information that could be extracted from aerial photos. For Truesdell, patterns that might otherwise be considered background noise or the mere vegetal context for more useful content held important information in their own right: "[the photographic interpreter [PI]] must be able to evaluate features that are not strictly military but which do have a bearing on various military aspects... our main interest and intent, as PIs, is to obtain as much information as possible and then to apply this information towards military usage."[17] For every aerial image that contained a military target, Truesdell reasoned that there was much more information to be gathered by interpreting the image's background vegetation. But Truesdell's photobotany wasn't just a call to appreciate the military significance of vegetation and to direct his colleague's attention to it; he was acknowledging a novel practice where botanical analysis and photographic interpretation merged into something messy, synthetic, and new.

Truesdell's call for a photobotanical analysis was informed by the work of O'Neill, Dutilly, and Hanson. In his role as an analyst at NPIC, Truesdell managed O'Neill's research for the ONR, and trained O'Neill and his team in techniques of photographic interpretation.[18] He witnessed how the requirements of photographic interpretation affected the standard methods of the botanists when they were used within a military context, and likewise, how PIs completely inverted their practices when operating with a new botanical awareness. Vegetation that had previously been seen by the PIs as mere background noise was now in the foreground. And yet, what they were looking *at* [vegetation] was not what they were looking *for* [information about the ground], and even the ground that was being photographed and analyzed [North America] was not the ground to which their interpretation would ultimately be applied [USSR]. Vegetation had become a component of the photo-communication channel through which the landscape was read and mapped. It was a proxy for the terrain that it obscured, and a proxy for remote territories that were politically inaccessible. It was *media*. As such, the natural landscape, visual representation, and geographic knowledge were fully entangled.

Cold War photobotany, as embodied in O'Neill's research, created an uncertainty about what aerial photographs of the landscape represented. Of course, no photograph is true and critical histories of photography have repeatedly challenged photographic claims of objectivity. Like many other representations, a photograph constructs its objects in highly particular ways, investing them with cultural assumptions and political intent.[19] Historian Robin Kelsey stated this most succinctly when he described photography as a "double index" that points at the object it depicts, and at the social and political milieu in which the photograph was created.[20] But despite their acknowledgment that a photograph's meaning is not neatly contained in its tones and textures, these histories largely assume that a photograph at least *resembles* the object that it represents – this resemblance is seemingly foundational to photography's ontology. Photobotany was an exception to this rule. By mobilizing botanical knowledge within their practices of photo reconnaissance, the ONR created a different form of representation where the depiction of a vegetal landscape created information about something else, somewhere else, and at a vastly different scale. As a result, these photographs say more about a Cold War mindset of proxy, inference, and geopolitical inaccessibility than they do about the landscape they seem to represent.

11 O'Neill, *Investigation of Methods: Part 3*, Plate V.

12 Ibid., Plate M3.

13 The use of the term "photomorphic" follows its usage in Robert W. Peplies & James D. Wilson, *Analysis of a Space Photo of a Humid and Forested Region: A Case Study of the Tennessee Valley*, USGS Interagency Report USGS-206 [US Geological Survey, 1970].

14 Arthème Dutilly, Maximilian Duman & Ernest Lepage, "Some Terrain Conditions in the Lowlands of the Subarctic Deducible from Air Photographs," in O'Neill, *Investigation of Methods: Part 3*, 3.1.

15 Ibid., M.2.

16 Ibid., Appendix 1.

17 Page Truesdell, "Research Aspects of Military Photo Interpretation," in *Selected Papers on Photogeology* [Research and Development Board Committee on Geophysics and Geography, 1953], 215, 216.

18 Also notable at this moment was the influence of Robert N. Colwell. Colwell was head of training at NPIC and contributed to the education of O'Neill's team. Perhaps more importantly, Colwell, a plant physiologist, was responsible for the first military use of the plant indicator concept in aerial photographic interpretation during WWII. His work in that context, and his relationship with the ONR, explains why the ONR would consider contracting botanists, like O'Neill, in the late 1940s and early 1950s. A detailed history of these relationships is explored by the author in *High Contrast: False Color Landscapes of the Cold War* [University of Texas Press, forthcoming].

19 Geoffrey Batchen, *Burning with Desire: The Conception of Photography* [MIT Press, 1997]; c.f. Richard Bolton [ed.], *Contest of Meaning: Critical Histories of Photography* [MIT Press, 1989].

20 Robin Kelsey & Blake Stimson [eds], *The Meaning of Photography* [Clark Art Institute, 2008], xi.

Opposite [from left]: Nahanni Valley vegetation indicating terrain conditions on sloped land; Nahanni Valley vegetation as depicted in high altitude aerial photography.

MAP 3 — THE EXPLOSION

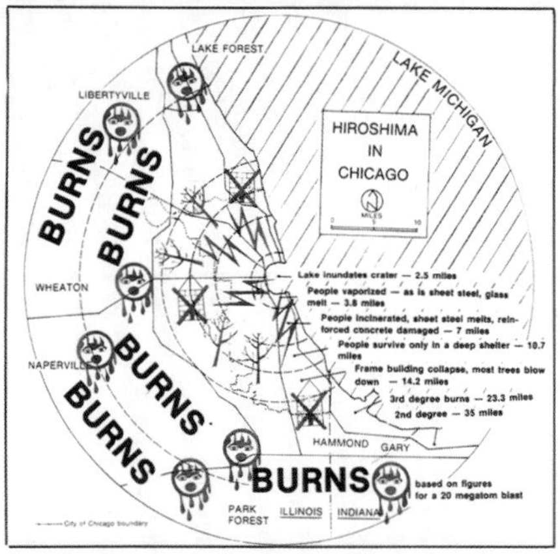

BURNS BURNS BURNS BURNS BURNS **BURNS**

LIBERTYVILLE • LAKE FOREST • LAKE MICHIGAN

WHEATON • NAPERVILLE • HAMMOND • GARY • PARK FOREST

HIROSHIMA IN CHICAGO
(20 megaton bomb)
MILES

Lake inundates crater – 2.5 miles
People vaporized – as is sheet steel, glass melt – 3.8 miles
People incinerated, sheet steel melts, reinforced concrete damaged – 7 miles
People survive only in a deep shelter – 10.7 miles
Frame building collapse, most trees blow down – 14.2 miles
3rd degree burns – 23.3 miles
2nd degree – 35 miles
based on figures for a 20 megaton blast

City of Chicago Boundary
ILLINOIS INDIANA

Look at what an H bomb would do to Chicago. The bulk of the inner city is destroyed directly by the blast, flat as a pancake except for the crater near ground zero. Cities as far away as Milwaukee, cross wind from the radiation might be safe, but cities downwind ever farther away into the State of Michigan, especially if there is a rainout, might expect many early deaths from radiation. And all this death is caused by a single bomb, a most unlikely optimistic assumption.

MAP 4 — THE FIRE-STORM

BLINDNESS BLINDNESS BLINDNESS BLINDNESS BLINDNESS **BLINDNESS**

LAKE FOREST • LAKE MICHIGAN • ELGIN • GENEVA • WHEATON • AURORA • JOLIET • PARK FOREST

RADIATION FIRE-STORM CRATER

HIROSHIMA IN CHICAGO
(20 megaton bomb)
MILES

20 miles / 16 miles / 16 miles / 20 miles

City of Chicago Boundary
ILLINOIS INDIANA

The heat from the conventional fires which will follow the nuclear destruction will produce its own terrible wind, like an outdoor blast furnace, and note that this second ring map is even larger than the first geography, the geography of Chicago's disappearance.

MAP 5 — NEW CHICAGO

S T A R V A T I O N

SURVIVERS SURVIVERS INVADING INVADING INVADERS RADIOACTIVE CORPSES

Rockford • Lake Forest • Dixon • Bloomington

HIROSHIMA IN CHICAGO
(20 megaton bomb)
MILES

40 miles / 20 miles / 16 miles / 16 miles / 20 miles / 40 miles

ILLINOIS INDIANA

RADIATION · SCORCHED · DYING · BLIND · INSANE · SICK

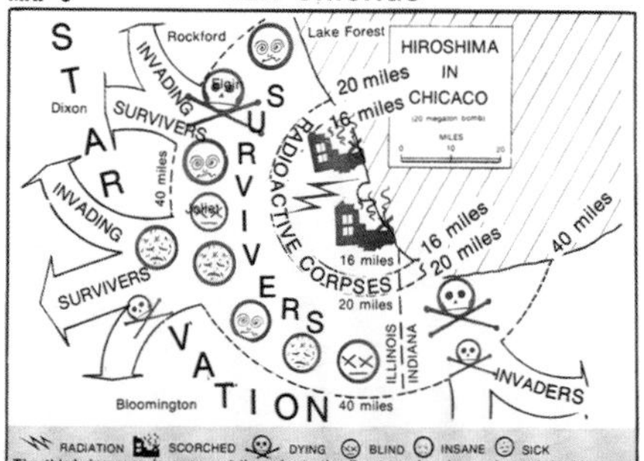

The third ring map is apparent the minute the firestorm has burned out. It is the geography of New Chicago which gradually fades away only after thousands of years. The new Port of Chicago, the Bay of Chicago, is surrounded by a "hot" ring. The corpses do not begin until after the edges of the fire storm is passed. The rings of the dead; blinded, crazed, dying-of-radiation sickness, finally give way to the largest ring of all, the ring of the starving. Even distant farmers without pesticides, fertilizer, horses or gasoline for farm machinery, might starve.

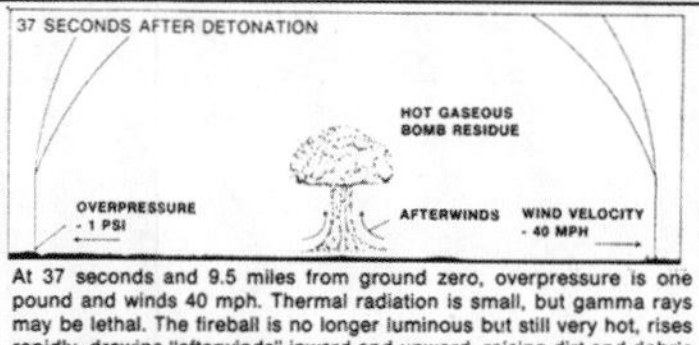

---

37 SECONDS AFTER DETONATION

HOT GASEOUS BOMB RESIDUE

OVERPRESSURE – 1 PSI
AFTERWINDS – 40 MPH

At 37 seconds and 9.5 miles from ground zero, overpressure is one pound and winds 40 mph. Thermal radiation is small, but gamma rays may be lethal. The fireball is no longer luminous but still very hot, rises rapidly, drawing "afterwinds" inward and upward, raising dirt and debris in the mushroom cloud stem.

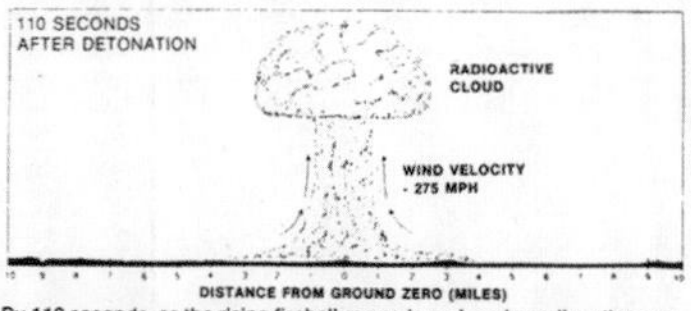

110 SECONDS AFTER DETONATION

RADIOACTIVE CLOUD
WIND VELOCITY – 275 MPH

DISTANCE FROM GROUND ZERO (MILES)

By 110 seconds, as the rising fireball expands and cools, radioactive particles condense into a cloud at a seven-mile height. After 10 minutes the cloud rises to about 14 miles. Wind later disperses the cloud, though precipitation may cause early (local) radioactive fallout. All told, the American Way of Life, is blown away in a flash.

"Effect and Dangers of Nuclear War." United Presbyterian Church in the U.S.A., 1981.

MAP 6 — SOUTHERN NEW ENGLAND AFTER

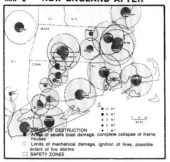

10 MT / 8 MT / 5 MT / 2 MT / 1 MT

ZONES OF DESTRUCTION
● Areas of severe blast damage, complete collapse of frame houses
○ Limits of mechanical damage, ignition of fires, possible extent of fire storms
□ SAFETY ZONES

F. Ervin, The New England Journal of Medicine, 1962

With a regional map of atomic war, as opposed to the "one-city-one-bomb" classic map, the problem of sustaining civilization takes on a realistic look. To where would the survivors flee? The "safe interiors" are merely interstices of the bombs, "half way to the next bomb". The earth's surface looks like what is left of a piece of flattened dough after being cut up by a cookie cutter.

MAP 7 — NUCLEAR DESTRUCTION BETWEEN LAKE DETROIT AND NIAGARA FALLS

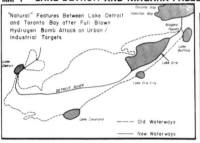

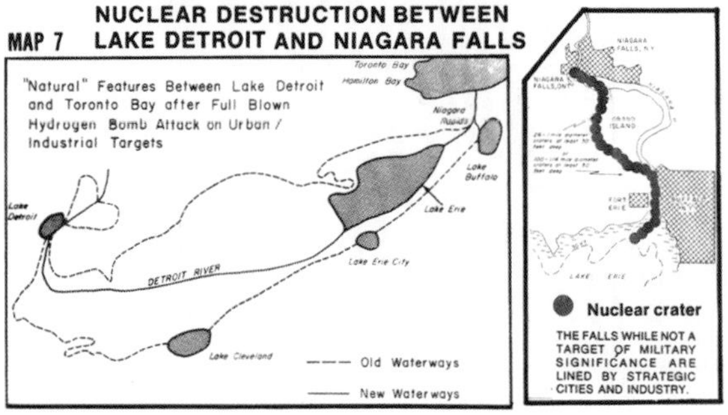

"Natural" Features Between Lake Detroit and Toronto Bay after Full Blown Hydrogen Bomb Attack on Urban / Industrial Targets

Lake Detroit • DETROIT RIVER • Lake Erie City • Lake Buffalo • Lake Cleveland

Old Waterways
New Waterways

NIAGARA FALLS, N.Y.

● Nuclear crater

THE FALLS WHILE NOT A TARGET OF MILITARY SIGNIFICANCE ARE LINED BY STRATEGIC CITIES AND INDUSTRY.

The nuclear geomorphology that might be produced around Lake Erie is startling, if the natural plug of Niagara Falls is blown out due to the heavy concentration of industrial targets at The Falls. The most evident feature would be the draining of the lake itself. Nuclear cratering could cause small deep lakes where none now exist such as a Lake Detroit, Lake Cleveland and so forth. Lake Ontario would not be drained so that bays would appear, "fine unnatural harbors" where major cities now stand such as Toronto Bay and Hamilton Bay.

MAP 8 — EDGE OF DEBRIS FROM THE FIFTH CHINESE NUCLEAR DETONATION

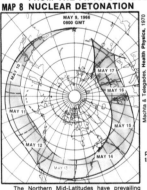

MAY 9, 1966 0800 GMT
MAY 17 / MAY 16 / MAY 15 / MAY 14 / MAY 13 / MAY 12 / MAY 11 / MAY 10

Machta & Telegades, Health Physics, 1970

The Northern Mid-Latitudes have prevailing Westerlies which circumnavigate the globe so it is possible, as in the Chinese test shown in the map, to sail the radiation around the planet and finally return home. The boomerang effect depicted in this map is like holding a rifle whose barrel is bent toward one's own head. But there are many examples of mass suicide being admired as patriotic such as the fight to the last man at Little Big Horn with General Custer. If one side in a war is willing to suicide collectively and the other is not; which side would win the war? If it does not seem patriotic to destroy your own nation, neither does it seem patriotic to not be willing to do so.

MAP 9 — PATRIOTIC POISONING

HELENA
APRIL 17 / APRIL 16 / APRIL 15 / APRIL 14
APRIL 9, 1965 1314 GMT

The successive areas covered by the nuclear cloud from a cratering event (Palanquin) on 14/04/65 determined by meteorological trajectories.

Machta & Telegades, Health Physics, 1970

The radioactive poisoning of your own nation by its own patriotic generals can only call into question their, or our collective species, sanity. "We have meant the enemy and he is us."

MAP 10 — THE NEUTRON BOMB

TORONTO • ETOBICOKE • SCARBOROUGH • E. YORK

RADIATION
DAMAGE TO REPRODUCTION
INTENSE HEAT
BLAST
DEAD IN 24 HRS
DEAD IN 6 DAYS
DEAD IN SEVERAL YEARS

15,840 – 3 miles
7,920
3,960
2,700
1,300
RAD II OF CIRCLES

SOURCE Toronto Sunday Star, March 5, 1978. Time, February, 1978.

"... a neutron bomb... would be... a poison gas abhorrent to civilized humanity, a monster that rather than kill would, in the current nuclear jargon, "juice" its victims. While many close range would die quickly, many others would linger on to a horrible death after days, weeks, or months of infernal torture."
W.L. Lawrence, "Nuclearism", Child Psychology, 1980.

MAP 11 — THREE MILE ISLAND

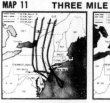

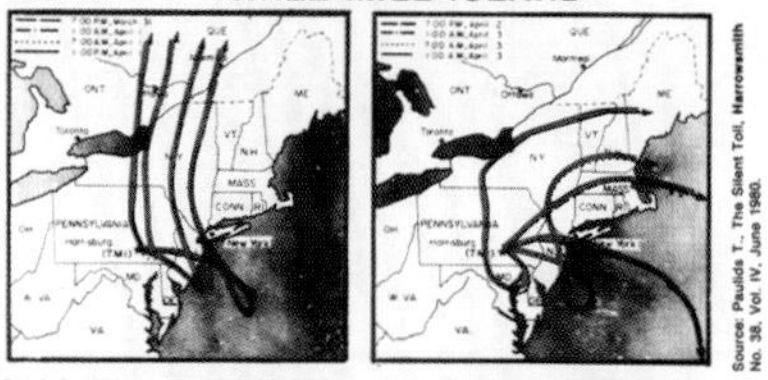

Early in the accident, on March 31 and April 1, the radioactive emissions were carried directly north across New York State and into Canada.

The prevailing winds over Three Mile Island blew from west to east, as indicated, with the plume pathways on April 2 and 3, 1979.

Source: Paulos T, The Silent Toll, Harrowsmith No. 38, Vol. IV, June 1980.

Occasionally something so dramatic happens that it changes history. Historians like to attribute all "historic events" to man, to his own actions, collective or individual, free willed or inevitable. But some historic events are not at all attributable to man. The eruption of Mt. Vesuvius and its consequence of burying alive Roman Pompeii was clearly a non-human historic event. Perhaps so was Three Mile Island. Perhaps Three Mile Island was a random inevitability that typifies nuclear physics. But again, in that nuclear power plans could be deliberately melted down by internal sabotage, then they are clearly historic events of the human made kind.

MAP 12 — NUCLEAR POISON GAS CLOUD

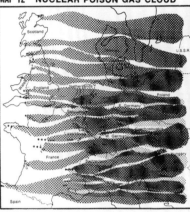

Scotland • U.S.S.R. • Poland • W. Germany • France • Spain

If you compare the map of nuclear reactors in Middle Europe, especially West Germany, with the map projecting atomic attack on Southern New England, how could the West German "peaceful" nuclear reactors possibly be put through an atomic war without melting them down? Nuclear war inevitably makes peaceful atomic power into a war weapon. It is not possible to miss the reactors. Perhaps West German military men calculated that the prevailing Westerlies would produce a poison gas cloud of converging plumes that might kill everyone, absolutely everyone, toward the east, including Poland for which the West professes so much sympathy.

MAP 13 — THE SEA OF CANCER

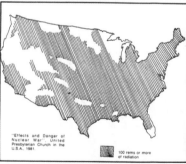

"Effects and Danger of Nuclear War." United Presbyterian Church in the U.S.A., 1981.

100 rems or more of radiation

In a full nuclear war, not only will most of the United States be washed in immediate radiation but even the white areas on the map are only safe in the sense that people in the open escape short term damage but not long term. The cancer is everywhere.

MAP 14 — THE MARCH OF DOOM

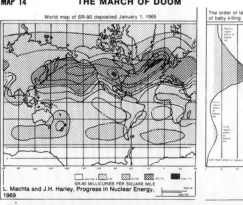

World map of SR-90 deposited January 1, 1965

The order of latitudes of baby killing

SR-90 MILLICURIES PER SQUARE MILE

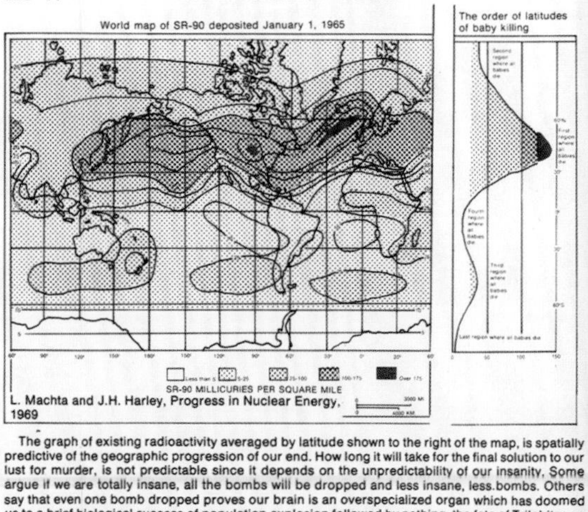

L. Machta and J.H. Harley, Progress in Nuclear Energy, 1969

The graph of existing radioactivity averaged by latitude shown to the right of the map, is spatially predictive of the geographic progression of our end. How long it will take for the final solution to our lust for murder, is not predictable since it depends on the unpredictability of our insanity, Some argue if we are totally insane, all the bombs will be dropped and less insane, less bombs. Others say that even one bomb dropped proves our brain is an overspecialized organ which has doomed us to a brief biological success of population explosion followed by nothing. the fate of Trilobites as revealed as fossils in the record of the rocks. The last babies that could be conceived and live borne will be at the South Pole, and then, not even there.

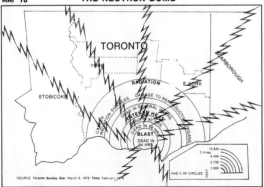

MATTHEW W. WILSON

CRITICALITY AS INTERPRETATION DECEPTION DISTORTION?

"One of the paradoxes of the latest technological revolution in cartography, involving the introduction of GIS, is that while it emphasizes images made by machines it also has the potential to broaden the disciplinary outlook by forging links with new subjects that use the same systems or contribute to their development."[1]

Matthew W. Wilson is associate professor of geography in the Department of Geography at the University of Kentucky and visiting scholar at the Center for Geographic Analysis at Harvard University. He is co-editor of *Understanding Spatial Media* and his most recent book is *New Lines* (2017). His current research examines early 20th-century thought on mapmaking and geographic education.

+ CARTOGRAPHY, GEOGRAPHY

The issue that confronts mapmaking today is not, perhaps, a complete *lack of critical perspective* on the part of designers and the publics that view such images, but rather, a *recognition that the form of criticality matters*, that criticality is not one-size-fits-all. It is significant then, now 30 years after the publication of Brian Harley's influential "Deconstructing the Map" and 20 years after James Corner's "The Agency of Mapping," that designers in the field of landscape architecture take stock of the forms of mapping and visualization that seek to propel new worlds.[2] Indeed, while new machines for the creation of images have proliferated in the time since these deconstructions, the forms of criticality remain unchanged: that images often disguise the techniques, politics, and biases of their making. Radical and critical mapmaking have become more-established modes of practice and thought, and yet, the possibilities to make a difference with novel and imminent technosocial relations are limited by increasingly skeptical publics as to the intent of such critically engaged images. I argue that to take up this issue is to attend to the provenance of criticality in GIS. In this essay, I consider this through two central figures: Brian Harley and his collaborator John Pickles.

On 27 December 1991, Ellen Hanlon from the University of Wisconsin-Milwaukee sent a single-page fax to the Department of Geography at the University of Kentucky, addressed to Professor John Pickles: "I have the unhappy task of informing you of Brian Harley's death on Dec. 20. You may already know this terrible news. I've called Peter Wissoker of Guilford Publications and I am sending all of Brian's files on this project to you."[3] Thus ended a relationship that had begun at least seven years prior. Wissoker was the acquisitions editor at Guilford, working with Brian and John on the front end of an edited book project that would alter the disciplinary landscape of anglophone geography; *Ground Truth: The Social Implications of Geographic Information Systems* was published in 1995, and the response was mixed.[4]

The discipline of geography was changing. Renewed emphases on technologies for geographical inquiry and representation were solidifying in the forms of new coursework and new degree programs in universities. As critical human geographers were debating the implications of poststructural and feminist interventions, the wider discipline took note of the rise of computational approaches in geographical study. Harley's and Pickles's interventions in these debates would later crystalize, alongside many other interlocutors, as a form of critical cartography and, later, critical GIS.[5] This critical approach would require both attention to the social and political implications of mapmaking and geospatial technologies and knowledge of *how* to make maps and to use GIS. Of course, the debates generated a plurality of opinions as to what kinds of technical knowledge were necessary and what kinds of implications were permissible to discuss. These uncomfortable times are perhaps well storied.[6] Indeed, there remains an urgency to engage critically, to both situate the practices of geographic representation and to intervene with the drawing of new lines. Therefore, in what follows, I ruminate on *Ground Truth*, by discussing the forms of criticality that encouraged Harley to reach out to Pickles and by proposing that these forms of critical thinking both created opportunities and limitations for the practices of critical mapmaking.

Harley earned his PhD in 1960, Pickles in 1983. It would be Pickles's interest in maps that have an explicit intent to change opinions ("propaganda maps") that initially caught Harley's attention in 1984.[7] Years later, in a letter to Harley in 1990, Pickles wrote, "In a sense I have used propaganda maps to get at the broader issues of interpretation/deception/distortion in the context of contemporary discourses about science."[8] They were corresponding about an edited collection, *Writing Worlds* by Trevor Barnes and Jim Duncan, in which they were both contributors. This collection would be published in 1992.[9] It is this interest in propaganda maps, and the parallel to debates about science, that animates my thinking about the provenance of criticality and the object of criticism. How might maps with explicit intent to change opinion operate in a similar field of relations to maps, more generally?

While we should read this statement as part of a genre of describing the scope of one's scholarship to a senior academic, Pickles's use of interpretation, deception, and distortion provides a useful vantage point. Both Pickles and Harley would note that they are not mapmakers (and certainly not GIS users). Maps, here propaganda maps, were artifacts that illustrated the socio-political capacities of geographic representation. It

was this approach to the study of maps and mapmaking that captured Harley's attention and propelled forward a writing project with Pickles to intervene in the technoscientific rewiring of the discipline. The question of what mapmaking is under new technological conditions moved toward the question of how mapmaking operates within society. And as Mike Goodchild would later reflect on *Ground Truth*, "GIScience would never again be quite the comfortable retreat for the technically minded that it had been in the past."[10]

To return to the culminating moments that emerge in *Ground Truth*—to ruminate on interpretation, deception, and distortion in thinking/practicing mapmaking—is to introduce questions about our understanding of criticality in mapmaking. I believe these culminating moments are important (however incomprehensive), especially as these partially set the conditions for discussion and debate within a discipline grappling with how to make adjustments amid a computational revolution in "the way we do things." Perhaps little has changed in 30 years. The resonance that these moments have in allied fields of the social sciences and humanities, in the computational sciences, and in planning and design—as this volume of *LA+* illustrates—is a reminder that the urgency of criticality is perhaps more simply a recognition that objectivity requires the strength of context and situation, and that strong objectivity is always about intervening to make change.[11]

Interpretation

Pickles's research on propaganda maps aligned with Harley's project to understand the underlying ideology of maps. Propaganda, by definition, exposes the explicit intent of the mapmaker: the ideology of the map is thinly disguised, perhaps. It is this thin disguise that allows scholars of cartography to best witness how maps cultivate an audience and extend a (political) position. In this time period of the late 1980s and 1990s, cartographic scholarship was enamored with behavioral and cognitive theories of graphic communication.[12] For Pickles then, "the cartographer and the map are at the centre of debates over technocracy and power in the modern world"; therefore, to consider maps as texts, instead of communicative vessels, is to witness their "influence [over] the social construction of reality" beyond the purely behavioral-cognitive.[13] Pickles moves quickly to show that explicitly propagandic maps are not exceptions to the wider body of maps and the practices of mapmaking. Instead, these propaganda maps are emblematic of the role of maps in society.

Here, interpretation, deception, distortion might be thought as a continuum of propagandist approaches to mapmaking, where interpretation is a practice (common to representation itself) that selects some aspects of a situation to be revealed, while leaving other aspects of that same situation absent and silent.[14] In this way, mapmakers construct representation through techniques that interpret the "real" and substitute

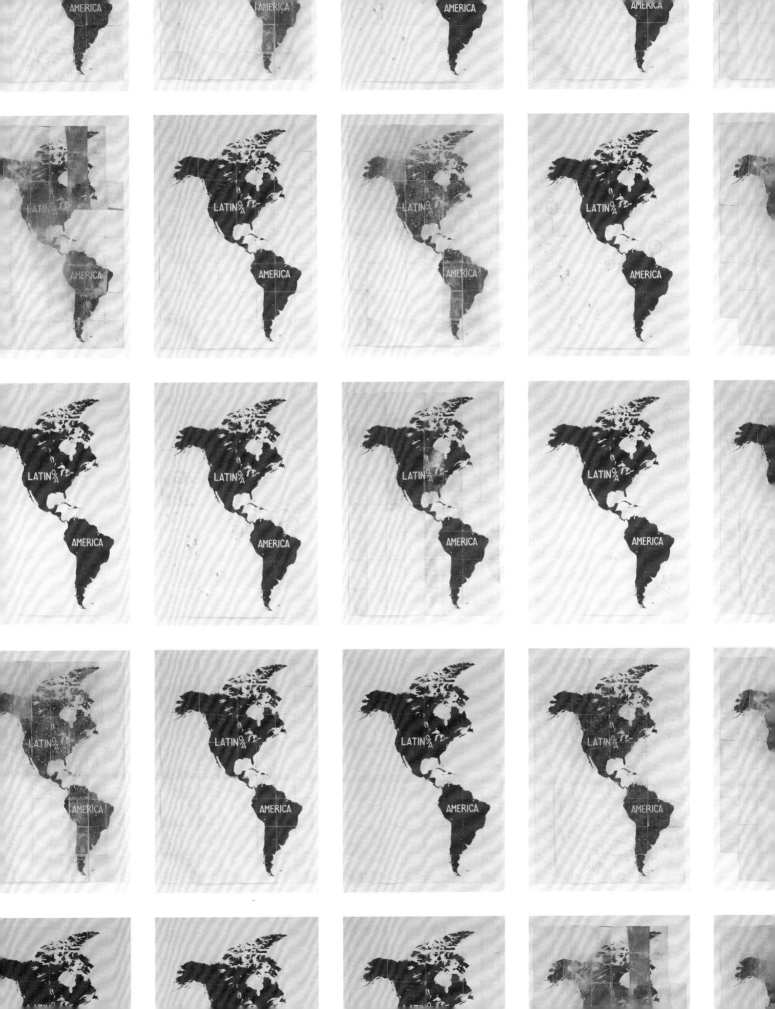

this situation with what becomes the represented: the map *becomes* the territory by disguising the practices that interpret that territory into a map.

Deception

This form of disguise becomes more pernicious and slippery, and yet further reveals the capacities of cartography, when we consider the deceptive potential of mapmaking (scientific, propagandic, as well as critical and radical). Deception implies another degree of intent beyond interpreting or selecting the "truth" of a situation for representation. These forms of propagandic maps (and perhaps indeed all maps, following Pickles) operate through controlled deception. Here, the map becomes a surface or interface through which selective interest slips (by accident or intention) into an explicitly narrow form of storytelling that reveals "a truth." However, this is a truth that would pale in comparison to a more "comprehensive" (read, "objective") mapmaking effort.

Interpretation and deception are glass-half-full, glass-half-empty perspectives on the cartographic enterprise. Either perspective is perhaps anathema to more dogmatic insistence on the objective ideals of mapmaking: the point is to limit the biases in practices of interpretation and never deceive, or so we are told. However, deception in maps is a form of trickery and is, in specific situations, a welcome end that justifies the means. How else might we squeeze the world into a flat framing device than to strategically deceive the user of the world's dynamisms, rounded trajectories, and distant simultaneities? How else might we begin to gather steam and insist on urgencies?

Distortion

All maps distort, but all maps distort in differing degrees. We might note here how even the selection of a map projection is a practice in distortion.[15] The point is to distort, but distort *well*. To insist that all maps distort is to introduce some productive ambiguity in mapmaking, including "critical" mapmaking. Pickles argues that the distinctions created for maps that are considered propaganda introduce some uneasy questions: "Are only those maps which use certain graphical techniques to create a distorted impression to be considered propaganda maps? Or are there certain categories of map *use* that constitute propaganda, while other uses do not? Are all maps propaganda maps?"[16] He continues, "the problem is not how to dissolve the distinction between propaganda maps and other maps, but how to work out whether we can establish any criteria of judgement once we recognize the discursive nature of texts such as maps."[17]

Distortion is inherent to mapmaking, a necessary step in the cartographic process. Distorting well, as the technologies of mediation evolve and morph, will require renewed innovation in design. It is around this necessity that an opportunity arises to link-up with practitioners and cartographic scholars of a behavioral-cognitive ilk. The rapid shifts in the attention economy will require new platforms and standards for engagement with maps. We must tinker and fail with maps in these situations, to assert new relevance in geographic representation amid a creeping toxicity in our media-rich society.

In a 10-page draft prospectus of a book proposal for Guilford's series: *Mappings: Society/Theory/Space*, sent in July of 1991 just five months before Harley's death, Pickles outlines a project with eight essays (the eventual book would have 10 essays and a preface), informing Harley that "[e]verything about the organization and structure of the book is up for grabs." The prospectus begins by discussing the scope of the text, in the context of a projected "35 to 40 percent growth" of a "GIS profession," that the book's collection of essays "are motivated in one way or another by a deep concern for the impacts of new unmediated technical practices in geography."[18] Harley and Pickles were concerned for the discipline of geography, viewing new technologies in mapmaking as potential assailants, while also concerned

1 J. Brian Harley, "Cartography, Ethics and Social Theory," *Cartographica* 27, no. 2 (1990): 21, fn 49.

2 J. Brian Harley, "Deconstructing the Map," *Cartographica* 26 (1989): 1–20; James Corner, "The Agency of Mapping: Speculation, Critique and Invention," in Denis E. Cosgrove (ed.), *Mappings* (Reaktion Books, 1999).

3 Fax dated 27 December 1991 from Ellen Hanlon to John Pickles, "Papers of Brian Harley," Personal Academic Correspondence: Pickles, John. Box 35. Maps, The British Library.

4 See Pickles's recollection of this in Jeremy W. Crampton & Matthew W. Wilson (eds), "Harley and Friday Harbor: A Conversation with John Pickles," *Cartographica* 50, no. 1 (2015): 28–36 doi: 10.3138/carto.50.1.06 as well as the special issue of *Transactions in GIS* organized by Michael Goodchild, "GIScience Ten Years After *Ground Truth*," *Transactions in GIS* 10, no. 5 (2006): 687–92. See also Nadine Schuurman & Geraldine Pratt, "Care of the Subject: feminism and critiques of GIS," *Gender, Place and Culture* 9, no. 3 (2002): 297. They write, "We have urged a change of attitude in critiques of GIS, from morally and intellectually superior outsider to critic who is more open about his/her complicities in shared circuits of power and intellectual traditions."

5 An overview of this history is reviewed by Nadine Schuurman as part of her doctoral research, see "Trouble in the Heartland: GIS and its critics in the 1990s," *Progress in Human Geography* 24, no. 4 (2000): 569–90.

6 I examine these storytellings and their importance for both an understanding of practice and of criticality in Matthew W. Wilson, *New Lines: Critical GIS and the Trouble of the Map* (University of Minnesota Press, 2017).

7 Letter dated 12 December 1984 from Brian Harley to John Pickles, "Papers of Brian Harley." Harley notes that he had seen mention of John's work on "propaganda maps and the creation of world views" in the *AAG Newsletter* of April 1984.

8 Letter dated 4 January 1990 from John Pickles to Brian Harley, "Papers of Brian Harley."

9 Trevor Barnes & Jim Duncan, eds. *Writing Worlds: Discourse, texts, and metaphors in the representation of landscape* (Routledge, 1992). This collection would also publish, posthumously, a version of Harley's "Deconstructing the Map."

10 Goodchild, "GIScience," 687.

Previous: A collection of Guias de Ruta (Route Guides) from travelers crossing the U.S.-Mexico border. These images are part of the *Latino/a America* works by artist Pedro Lasch.

for society, as new technologies of geography and cartography were being enrolled in new forms of surveillance and control. That Harley originally contacted Pickles in 1984 to discuss propaganda maps as "the creation of world views" underlines their shared perspective on maps: maps are objects that enable, produce, stage, enact, or reveal worlds. However, as neither would offer this perspective as map*makers*, the criticism was perhaps more narrowly received (a fault not uniquely their own).[19] Today, we might note that their concerns were well-founded, that geospatial technologies have proliferated as a variety of seemingly invisible and conspicuous algorithms, devices, technologies, and practices that intervene in the everyday.

In conclusion, I am not suggesting interpretation, deception, distortion as *the* approaches to criticality in mapmaking. Indeed, there are other ways to think and practice intervention in and with maps.[20] However, I suggest that to understand the ossification of the critical in mapping and perhaps in wider fields of geographic inquiry (to include design, digital humanities, environmental and health justice, etc.) is to understand the discursive pressure placed upon the map. That the audiences for such a critical mapmaking impulse might read such efforts as politically motivated and biased is part of the challenge of criticality. The point is not that critical cartography and critical GIS should produce maps that appropriately foreground their interpretative position, their controlled deception, and their managed distortion, but that *all* mapmaking efforts interpret, deceive, and distort. This is the responsibility that comes of being responsive. That an important book like *Ground Truth* both beguiled and repelled a generation of scholars, activists, and practitioners is a reminder that criticality and criticism in mapmaking begins and ends with a question of the critic's relationship to the object of criticism. To make a map is to begin with its agency;[21] to make a map critically is to apply yet further pressure on that agency, to nudge the lines of our maps into domains that make a difference. In one of his last essays on cartography and ethics, Harley's conclusion is foreboding still: "The real crisis will be when the mapmakers finally cease to live within their maps and when the age of technicity is all that is left for cartography."[22]

11 Here, I lean on feminist critiques of science, see Sandra Harding, "Rethinking Standpoint Epistemology: What is 'Strong Objectivity?'" *The Centennial Review* 36, no. 3 (1992): 437–70.

12 This variant of cartographic scholarship might substitute *Ground Truth* for Alan MacEachren, *How Maps Work: Representation, Visualization, and Design* (Guilford Press, 1995).

13 John Pickles, "Texts, Hermeneutics and Propaganda Maps (1992)," in *Writing Worlds*, 194.

14 J. Brian Harley, "Silences and Secrecy: The Hidden Agenda of Cartography in Early Modern Europe," *Imago Mundi* 40 (1988): 57–76.

15 Jeremy W. Crampton, "Cartography's Defining Moment: The Peters Projection Controversy, 1974–1990," *Cartographica* 31, no. 4 (1994): 16–32.

16 John Pickles, "Texts, Hermeneutics and Propaganda Maps (1992)," 199.

17 Ibid., 200.

18 Letter Pickles to Harley, 19 July 1991 with prospectus, copy shared by Pickles, including annotations by Harley. The title *Ground Truth* was not mentioned in this proposal. The eight essays proposed in the prospectus were to be written by Pickles, Wolfgang Natter, Joni Seager, Derek Gregory, Harley, Michael Curry, Michael Goodchild, and Peter Taylor. Only essays by Curry, Goodchild, and Taylor (as well as Pickles and Harley) would make it into *Ground Truth*.

19 I discuss similar contemporary pressures on the doing of mapmaking in a chapter titled "But Do You Actually *Do* GIS?" in Wilson, *New Lines*.

20 For instance, see Alexis Bhagat & Lize Mogel (eds), *An Atlas of Radical Cartography* (Journal of Aesthetics and Protest Press, 2008); Trevor Paglen, *Blank Spots on the Map: The Dark Geography of the Pentagon's Secret World* (Dutton, 2009); Tera Hatfield, Jenny Kempson & Natalie Ross, *Seattleness: a cultural atlas* (Sasquatch Books, 2018).

21 Corner concludes, "What remains unseen and unrealized across seemingly exhausted grounds becomes actualized anew with the liberating efficacy of creatively aligned cartographic procedures," 252.

22 Harley, "Cartography, Ethics and Social Theory," 19.

IN CONVERSATION WITH
WILLIAM RANKIN

William Rankin's recent book, *After the Map*, traces the history of three global projects–the International Map of the World [1891–1986], the Universal Transverse Mercator [1940–1965], and the Global Positioning Systems [GPS]–to demonstrate the emerging logic of the grid as a technology of geographic cohesion and consolidation. He argues that electronic navigation systems have superseded representational mapping, the result of which is a radical shift in how we understand the nature of territory. Rankin, who is both an historian and a cartographer, spoke with **Karen M'Closkey + Keith VanDerSys** about his book, his favorite maps, and what's on the horizon.

+ Your book is provocatively titled *After the Map*, which could imply that maps are obsolete. Is this the case or is it only certain institutional forms of cartography that are obsolete, or superseded by technologies like GPS, where coordinate systems take precedence over images?

The "the" in my title is important – it's *After the Map* rather than *After Maps*. The key point of the book is not that there's a shift away from maps–today there are perhaps more digital maps produced in a single year than there were paper maps drawn in any previous decade of human history–but rather that we should ask where authoritative knowledge is lodged. Where is the project of universalism? Where do you look when you need the truth of space? Formerly, authority was lodged in maps. They were the preferred technology for making space legible, manageable, and knowable, but their status changed dramatically over the 20th century. Maps become less authoritative. They started to be questioned, not just by critical theorists and humanists, but by practitioners themselves.

+ The critiques of mapping that arose in geography in the 1980s and '90s were incredibly influential to landscape architecture. James Corner draws on this important body of work in his 1999 essay "The Agency of Mapping," which came only 10 years after J.B. Harley's now canonical "Deconstructing the Map." The word "critique" has fallen away, at least in our field. What are key differences between critical cartography and radical cartography, the latter of which is the title of your website?

I have a real respect for that work from the '80s and '90s. Many of those scholars wanted to offer a radical new take on cartography, and they pushed back against a naïve understanding of maps as documents of perfect objective truth. But in the book I argue that this critique was actually more like a solidification of a view that was already widely held by practitioners themselves. Historically, I think we see the internal erosion of the idea of a perfect totalizing map happening alongside or even before the critique, rather than the critique coming first. Also, I think most of that work from the '80s and '90s stops a bit short. It says that maps are tools of power and therefore bad. But this only gets us so far, because it doesn't help us imagine a world where maps, or power, operate any differently. And as experts–even as humanistic experts–we're all, in some way, still implicated in these forms of power.

For me the distinction between a critical approach to maps and my radical cartography project is that mine tries to respond to maps with maps rather than just with critique. And that's harder in some sense. It's relatively straightforward to point out all the ways that a map might be misleading or a tool of power or part of a colonial project. This critique is important and true and needs to be said, but even though the critique is convincing it hasn't really done much to dislodge the hegemonic status of mainstream maps, which are hegemonic not because of their hidden ideology but because of how they represent the world and how they're able to be used.

+ GIS is the most prevalent mapping tool in our field. It was definitely a subject of those critiques, in particular how quantitative the mapping had become. Are there limitations in using GIS in the mapping that you do or does your approach to GIS facilitate a reconception of where authority is lodged?

GIS is both really helpful and really loaded with assumptions that need to be rejected. The way that data is encoded in GIS usually suggests a default form of visualization. For example, it's very easy to make a choropleth map from online census data, but using that same data to make other kinds of maps requires real effort. And it's almost impossible for GIS to make a flow map. Yet a flow map is not an exotic form of visualization! If you look at books or magazines from before computers, flow maps are everywhere. So I try not to ask "what can I do with GIS," but rather "what kind of map do I want to make?" It's instructive to think about what kinds of basic moves have suddenly become difficult. Old maps were often tools of power, of course, but they can also be far more experimental, visually, than what's being made today.

+ Are there any eras or types of mapping that you look at in particular?

I have a huge digital collection of medieval maps, both from Europe and the Islamic world. And I love them because they really challenge the idea that we start with an empty world and then fill it up with better and better data over time. These medieval maps are *full* of stuff. They're full of animals and people and plants and stories and history. And they make you realize, especially the Islamic maps, that the perfect exactitude of the map is negotiable. They're incredibly abstract and very evocative, even poetic. I like letting go of the idea that we're at the bleeding edge of the latest innovations in data visualization. I like thinking of maps more in terms of argument and emotion. I also have a fondness for those 19th-century atlases with comparative drawings of all the rivers and mountains and waterfalls of the world, which can also get quite abstract. They carry some obvious colonial baggage, but they also make space for the reader's subjectivity and emotional response. They show an enthusiasm and a level of embellishment that I find really refreshing.

+ You've said elsewhere that your aim in practicing radical cartography is to reimagine boundaries. In our work as landscape architects, one of the most persistent and problematic boundaries is that between land and water. This simple division—codified in maps and datasets and the institutions that produce them—has profoundly shaped our settlement patterns. Have you seen a particular example of how we can overcome some of those land-water boundaries, which are so easily reinforced?

Yes, it's very hard to map the blurry boundary between land and water when the data that's being created, at almost every scale, shows just a single thin line. I'm reminded of the mapping that was initiated by the Inuit of northern Canada in the 1970s to make a land claim against the Canadian government. They hired anthropologists to interview almost every Inuit hunter in the Arctic about where they remembered finding particular species: caribou, moose, narwhal, ptarmigan, and so on. These memories would document the spatial extent of Inuit culture. The finished maps were produced by mainstream cartographers—they weren't made by the Inuit themselves—but they end up being almost illegible, in a wonderful sort of way, because when you overlay 20-something colored blobs on top of a standard topographic map, mixing land and marine species together, the line between land and water gets radically dissolved, at times almost entirely erased. And so the maps show a really different understanding of what space is, what territory is. It's a fluid expanse of earth and ice and water and snow; it's not just solid land that stops at a sharp coastline. Those maps were really important for forcing the Canadian federal government away from their old way of managing resources, with one agency for land and another for water. The

Inuit pushed them into creating a single agency, with Inuit representation, to manage wildlife across land and water together.

We always need to ask whether it's better to make knowledge legible to power or whether it's better to remain invisible. But the project wasn't just about putting Indigenous knowledge on a Western-style map. Mapping Inuit memory directly challenged some of the assumptions of Western territoriality. The final land-claims agreement wasn't perfect by any means—Inuit today still debate its shortcomings—but it was seen as a real improvement, a real victory. A lot of the literature about Indigenous counter-mapping is about the search for a perfectly Indigenous form of cartography, with as much of the mapping as possible left in non-Western, non-expert hands. But the Inuit project was a more hybrid effort – and its effects were, too.

+ You mentioned the issue of visibility and bringing awareness to what might otherwise be overlooked. Another such example is the mapping of the ocean floor – less than 5% has been mapped with a high level of detail. There is both excitement and trepidation about the Seabed 2030 proposal to map the entire ocean floor in the next decade: it could facilitate exploitation by mining and fossil fuel industries, or it could initiate greater protective regulations of these yet unseen resources. Are there times when not making aware might be a more productive strategy?

There are a lot of examples of the benefits of invisibility and there are definitely tradeoffs to mapping. Making yourself more legible, at least in the idiom of mainstream cartography, often means giving up a degree of spatial and temporal flexibility, where, for example, spaces can be multiply claimed and occupied, with decisions made at the local level rather than in some distant center of power. In the end, I don't think we should make any blanket assumptions about which is the right strategy, and we certainly shouldn't assume that more visible is always better. Instead, the decisions have to rest with the people who have the most at stake. And we have to accept that they might make choices that we, as outside experts, disagree with.

I also think about those expeditions in California to measure the tallest trees, the oldest trees, the most massive trees. We have very detailed information about those trees, but we don't know where they are. Their locations aren't published in order to protect them. This is another strategy in between perfect visibility and perfect invisibility.

+ It is also a question of who has access to, or who is making decisions about, what is and isn't accessible and visible.

I think that's the right question to ask—who is making these decisions—rather than asking what the right answer is for all projects.

+ You use the term "geo-epistemology" in your book to describe the ways in which tools produce certain kinds of knowledge. Does this notion of geo-epistemology arise with the aforementioned critiques of mapping or does it connote something quite different?

If you look at the scholarship on maps, there's often a sense that maps are a distinct, self-contained historical phenomenon and that we can understand the history of mapping through time without considering other types of geographic knowledge that aren't maps. (We talk about "the history of cartography," not "the history of geographic knowledge.") Geo-epistemology is my way of resisting this tendency. It makes it clear that maps are just one form of knowledge, with many competitors. In the book, I focus on GPS and other pointillist coordinate systems. My interest is still in the state and other large institutions—on forms of legibility and management from afar—and I use the term in order to talk about this new coordinate-based knowledge that isn't captured by maps. But things like directional signage, embodied experience, and collective memory are also forms of geo-epistemology.

+ Does geo-epistemology share commonalties with John Pickles's phrase "geoscopic regimes," or that of the God's-eye view of geographic knowledge during Western enlightenment?

Yes, it does, though a lot of research since Pickles has challenged the idea that this is a fundamentally Western project – we can actually see very similar projects in China, Japan, and elsewhere. It's important to recognize, even starting in the early modern period, that there's a more global history here of a certain kind of state apparatus, rather than just a "Western worldview," that relies on new forms of knowledge and management. This recent work also highlights all the other forms of knowledge within the Western tradition–the other geo-epistemologies–that are not map-like, or even all that "scopic." It's not the case that everyone living in Europe or its settler colonies always thinks about space through maps. That's just not true.

+ Unlike the distanced view of the "geoscopic," one of the elements that you characterize in your book is that the spatial paradigm of GPS implies a type of embeddedness. How does this change our geographic perspective?

For the user, the global system of GPS doesn't *feel* global at all; it doesn't encourage zooming out from the map, but rather zooming in to real-world points. It's a fundamentally localizing technology, and what makes it global is simply that the user can get their location anywhere in the world, regardless of what country they're in or whether they're on land or at sea. So the experience of GPS is actually not an experience of the globe as a whole; it's an experience of local knowledge without boundaries. And that, in turn, is a really different way of thinking about what global or planetary might mean.

Another point I highlight in the book is that there's almost nothing that's truly global. The only institution I found that's really trying to act globally is the US Navy, mostly because of nuclear submarines. The USSR copies the Navy's systems, but otherwise, the Air Force, the Army, other countries' militaries, commercial airlines, fishing, shipping, the UN, and so on down the line – none of these are really global. They have particular *regional* intensities. And I think it's important to see that the global project is just not that meaningful for most activities. Most things are about regional fluidity rather than global totality.

+ That's a point you highlight in the first part of your book, which describes the International Map of the World (IMW), an effort involving participation, in some way, by most countries. The project began in the 1890s and ceased by the 1980s due to skepticism about its value. But now there's a similar geographic desire by companies like Google or Esri.

The fundamental assumption of the IMW was that territorial states were the building blocks of the world, both spatially and epistemologically. Each country would contribute knowledge of its own territory, and that would create the final authoritative record of the planet. So it's not just that the map is divided into pastel-colored shapes, but that this jigsaw-puzzle logic shapes the very way we come to know the Earth at all.

Google and OpenStreetMap and Esri are very different kinds of institutions. Yes, the overall goal is still to collect knowledge from around the world into a single repository, but unlike with the IMW, there's no sense that territorial states are the foundation. Knowledge is constructed in lots of different ways at once – from bottom-up crowdsourcing and commercial vendors as much as from official government surveys. So it's important to see that the demise of the IMW wasn't just about the shift from paper to digital – it was about the political organization of knowledge. In fact, even for digital mapping there were attempts to sustain IMW-like projects – but they failed, too.

+ To follow up on that: is the prevalence of GPS impacting how we understand scale? In a universal coordinate system, like GPS, you're somewhat simultaneously local and global – you can always find yourself at a local point within a global space. This differs from traditional cartography where everything is about an increment of scale, a division of space.

Matthew Edney has a nice chapter on the mythology of scale in his recent book, *Cartography: The Ideal and Its History*. He describes the idea of a continuous spectrum of scale–where a local map is fundamentally the same sort of thing as a world map, just at a different scale–as one of the core fictions of modern cartography. And we see this online, for sure, with our little slider bars that let us zoom in and out, as if it's the same kind of mapping all the way up and down. His critique is expansive, and I think it's convincing. We really shouldn't think of all cartography as a single project across all scales, unified by what Chris Tong calls the "world zoom." Local maps and world maps are really very different sorts of things, and regional maps aren't "in between" – they're again doing something distinct, culturally and politically. And I think you're right that GPS challenges in some important way this assumption about the infinite scalability of experience and knowledge. GPS is multi-scalar, but it's not about zooming.

+ Is there anything that you're excited about that you're working on right now?

Yes. I'm taking my Radical Cartography website and writing a book from it. It'll bring my own mapping work into conversation with the last 200 years of mapping and visualization. I'm trying to get at some of the ideas we talked about earlier, about how to make a cartography that doesn't accept all the assumptions baked into our data, that questions some of the values of GIS and the rules of "dataviz," but that doesn't reject the map as an unredeemable tool of power. How can we make space for the values of uncertainty, ambiguity, and subjective experience, while still making maps? And how do we take the humanist critique of maps and turn it into a positive project – one that actually results in different kinds of maps?

LISA PARKS

VERTICAL MEDIATION AT STANDING ROCK

Lisa Parks is professor of comparative media studies and science, technology, and society at MIT, and is a 2018 MacArthur Fellow. Parks is author of *Cultures in Orbit: Satellites and the Televisual* (2005) and *Rethinking Media Coverage: Vertical Mediation and the War on Terror* (2018), and co-editor of *Life in the Age of Drone Warfare* (2017), *Signal Traffic: Critical Studies of Media Infrastructures* (2015), and *Down to Earth: Satellite Technologies, Industries and Cultures* (2012).

✚ MEDIA STUDIES, PUBLIC POLICY, TECHNOLOGY

Between March 2016 and February 2017 demonstrators gathered on the lands of the Standing Rock Sioux Nation to protest the construction of the 1,172-mile-long Dakota Access oil pipeline (DAPL) by Energy Transfer Partners, a Fortune 500 oil and natural gas company. The protests attracted thousands of Indigenous Americans and non-indigenous allies and made global news headlines as the activists, who called themselves "water protectors," engaged in a series of standoffs with law enforcers and private security firms. The water protectors' opposition to the pipeline was related to its routing through sacred tribal lands and beneath the Missouri and Mississippi rivers, as well as under Lake Oahe, a primary water source near the Standing Rock Sioux Nation's territory.

An October 18, 2016 PowerPoint presentation by Tiger Swan, a private security firm hired by Energy Transfer Partners to monitor DAPL protesters, featured an image of a gorilla in the clouds watching over the Standing Rock camp. The image, which appeared at the end of a daily intelligence update, projects Tiger Swan's omniscience and invincibility through this overlord figure who monitors the tiny water protectors below. I begin with this image description not only to point out Tiger Swan's quirky and belittling tone, but also to signal the importance of the *vertical field*—that continuous space from orbit to underground—and the power relations that have been mobilized through it in the battle to protect water at Standing Rock. Much of what we see and know about our world is predicated on the capacity to control the vertical field and the satellites and aircraft that move through it. Yet, many disciplines, including landscape architecture, often overlook the integral role of these technologies shaping understandings of global and local geographies and environments.

That the civilian drone is absent in Tiger Swan's audacious vision is telling, as the technology became a vital tool during the Standing Rock protests that enabled activists to create new forms of tactical media.[1] For American Indian communities, *indigenous media* have always been *tactical*. Media ranging from smoke signals to films to drum beats materialize a history of tactical media in North America that long precedes the digital era. By approaching Indigenous American drone media as *tactical* I want to consider them as part of a broader history of practices that emerged in response to settler-colonialism, and,

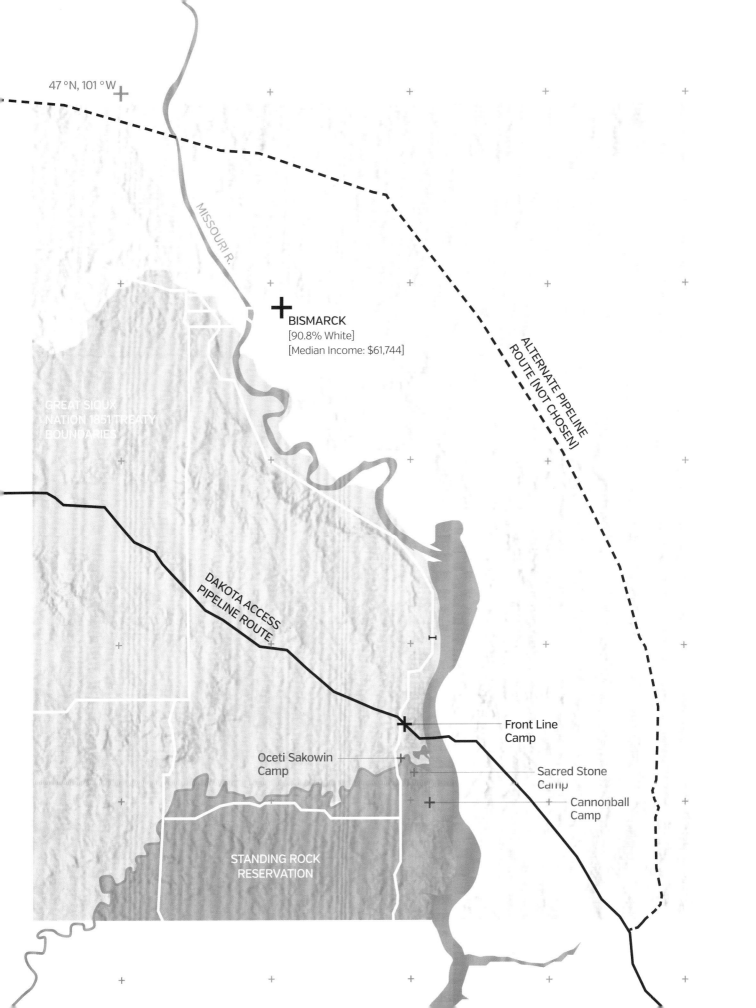

47°N, 101°W

MISSOURI R.

✚ BISMARCK
[90.8% White]
[Median Income: $61,744]

ALTERNATE PIPELINE
ROUTE [NOT CHOSEN]

GREAT SIOUX
NATION 1851 TREATY
BOUNDARIES

DAKOTA ACCESS
PIPELINE ROUTE

Front Line
Camp

Oceti Sakowin
Camp

Sacred Stone
Camp

Cannonball
Camp

STANDING ROCK
RESERVATION

at the same time, suggest that the concept of "tactical media" should be understood as a dynamic site of differential inflection, shaped by diverse cultural experiences and histories. It is also important to recognize that tactical media, especially those of Indigenous Americans, also have built within them implicit languages that are not intelligible to all, and are articulated with what Gerald Vizenor calls "survivance" – native presence that "remains obscure, elusive and imprecise" yet works to renounce "domination, tragedy and victimry."[2]

In this essay I approach Indigenous Americans' tactical drone videos as *vertical mediations* – audiovisual discourses that enact, materialize, or infer conditions or qualities of the vertical field.[3] These mediations demonstrate what is happening in the air, spectrum, or orbit, and how those happenings impact life on Earth. In doing so, they render intelligible material conditions and power relations of the vertical field, in the stretch of space from the air to underground. As Caren Kaplan crucially suggests, "airspaces," which include the vertical, are often ambiguous and "are produced by assemblages of human and machine and can be apprehended through a broad array of material objects, elements, infrastructures, practices, and operations."[4] The analysis in this essay is intended to draw further critical awareness to the relations between vertical power, drone technologies, and publics, and to highlight the surveillance strategies and discourses of law enforcers and private security firms who criminalize civilian drone use by activists. The anti-DAPL protests expose state forms of vertical power that are immanent with the globalization of civilian drone technology, and make tribal sovereignty claims over air space more urgent.

Drone Warriors

Dean Dedman, Jr, also known as Shiyé Bidzííl (Hunkpapa Lakota and Diné), began using his civilian drone at Standing Rock in March 2016. Myron Dewey (Newe-Numah/Paiute-Shoshone) joined the effort in August 2016. The two were celebrated for their drone media work throughout the protests, and became known as "drone warriors" in the camps.[5] Though there were other activist drone pilots, I focus on the work of Dedman and Dewey because their drone videos circulated widely, became integral to their activism, provoked police action, and won film awards.[6] In his book *Through Indigenous Eyes*, Dedman recounts the first flight of his Chinese-made DJI Phantom 3 – purchased for 2500 dollars with his tax return. On March 11, less than one week after purchasing his drone, Dedman formed a drone video business called Drone2bwild, and by March 28 posted his first anti-DAPL drone video–*Dakota Access Protest. The Run for Water*–on his Drone2bwild Facebook page. Between March 2016 and January 2017, he recorded over 100 drone videos of various activities at Standing Rock – from gatherings at camps to phases of the pipeline's construction, from incursions on sacred sites to law enforcers' activities. He live streamed and archived these videos on Facebook and Unicorn Riot, and posted longer videos on YouTube and other platforms.[7]

When Dedman describes his drone he emphasizes its material relation to his community and the environment, characterizing it as a "water protector" that "watches skies, and protects the land and the water." He explains that drone warriors tie tobacco and sage onto their drones in order to protect them, and insists drones have a soul.[8] His first anti-DAPL video–*Dakota Access Protest. The Run for Water*–features drone footage of tribal members running, walking, horse-riding, and driving across the Missouri River in a run for water. Dedman's drone hovers above as bodies make their way across the bridge as the water looms in the background. The perspective emphasizes the vastness of the water compared to the small bodies, and the time it takes for these bodies and vehicles to move across it. Multiple times, water runners look up and acknowledge the drone as a flying ally. Another drone video by Dedman dated October 24, 2016–*Drone2bwild vs. DAPL Security*–showcases Energy Transfer's massive DAPL construction site. This drone footage uniquely communicates the scale and impact of this infrastructural extension as the drone soars above a long stretch of pipeline excavation sites, grazed areas soon to become drilling platforms, scattered equipment, and connected bulldozed roadways. The view also hovers above law enforcers who are stationed along the DAPL site and captures officers shooting at Dedman's drone 10 different times, signaling the power and volatility of tactical drone media.

Reflecting on his videos, Dedman stresses his use of the drone to spotlight often ignored Indigenous American protests, claiming,

> I have captured the world's attention. Using just my drone has been very beneficial to my Native people across NDN country and beyond. It really does feel good to be a part of something that will forever capture the eyes of the world. Big media has yet to shed light on what's been going on here at the front lines of the Standing Rock reservation. But here I am with this little Phantom 3 Advanced, flying around, filming as it happens. The resistance of my people and destruction of my earth. It really does hurt me to see DAPL digging into her and mining her spirit.[9]

Dedman's videos not only garnered world attention, but also drew thousands more protestors to Standing Rock. As Dedman puts it, "The drone gave a better perspective of how the movement was evolving...That's why they came. They wanted to be a part of what they were seeing visually. These drones brought a lot of attention. The drones stepped it up a notch."[10] Drones, in other words, not only *represented* the protests; their verticality actively transformed conditions on the ground, compelling people to gather and move in certain directions and to do certain things. For instance, Dedman instructed protestors to "bring HUGE SIGNS WITH BIG BOLD ANTI-PIPELINE MESSAGES SO THAT THE DRONE WILL BE ABLE TO SEE THE SIGNS CLEARLY."[11]

As drone videos expanded the protests they bolstered police presence in the area as well. In August 2016, Dedman explained

Previous: "Protectors Not Protestors" photograph by Joe Brusky of the Overpass Light Brigade.

Top: Myron Dewey with his drone.

Bottom: Dean Dedman Jr with his drone.

to his followers on social media, "I'm trying my best to get drone footage for everyone, but they've been scrambling all our signals."[12] Law enforcers interrupted drone activism using spectrum interference, which prevented transmissions between the drone and controller. Myron Dewey, who began his drone activism under the name Digital Smoke Signals has explained that drone interference was not limited to scrambling: police confiscated and shot at drones as well. Dewey live streamed his Standing Rock drone videos on Facebook for months, and carefully narrated some of them so that "relatives"–Indigenous elders–could understand what was happening around the area. He also live streamed an October 8, 2016 incident in which he "feared for his life" as 17 unbadged officers pulled his car over, questioned him, and confiscated his drone.[13] Activist drone media had apparently become too tactical. A criminal complaint charged Dewey with using his DJI Phantom 4 drone to stalk two private security workers, who felt "frightened, intimated, and harassed" after Dewey posted a live feed on Facebook called "DAPL security."[14]

Despite signal interference and confiscation, Dewey and Dedman's drone videos continued and became increasingly focused on *providing cover* above water protectors as police encounters and activities escalated. On October 27, 2016 Dewey compiled footage from multiple drones that could not be live streamed because of a "media blackout." When he later posted the material on Facebook Dewey explained to relatives what kinds of confrontations were happening. He described, for instance, drone views of two men on horseback chased by police ATVs across a sacred burial site, as well as mass arrests and possible beatings at the "sacred fire" camp after police reportedly destroyed the "sacred tipi," pulled people out of a sweat lodge, and disrupted protestors in prayer. Dewey then discusses drone views of pipeline development sites, where drone videos are used not to grow and amplify the protest, but to monitor police pursuits and maneuvers occurring simultaneously throughout the camps and to formulate collective responses to them.

Some of Dewey's most important drone footage was recorded on the night of November 20, 2016, when police sprayed protestors with water in below freezing temperatures. Though violating FAA rules for civilian drone operations, which preclude flights at night, Dewey's drone captured views of water cannons blasting protestors at close range. These tactical drone media were used to document possible human rights violations, and at one point the water cannons almost blasted Dewey's drone out of the air.

Given that tribal members were blocked from accessing their own lands, the drone's visual mobility became all the more important, as it enabled Indigenous Americans and their allies to witness, gather evidence, and organize from sky to ground. People came together through and around drone views; these views and their creators inspired and gave expression to a tactical media formation interweaving practices of activism, journalism,

1 Media scholars have conceptualized tactical media in various ways, emphasizing opportunistic works, sometimes made with low-tech or DIY gadgets, designed to orchestrate media-based interventions and disturbances. As Geert Lovink writes, the concept of tactical media plays with "the ambiguity of more or less isolated groups or individuals, caught in the liberal-democratic consensus, working outside the safety of the Party or Movement, in a multi-disciplinary environment full of mixed backgrounds and expectations." It also involves "the art of getting access, hacking the power and disappearing at the right moment." Geert Lovink, *Dark Fiber* [MIT Press, 2002]. Rita Raley stresses the temporality and ephemerality of tactical media and crucially observes, "It is not simply that interventions by tactical media may disturb but that the outcomes of those disturbances remain uncertain and unpredictable." Rita Raley, *Tactical Media* [University of Minnesota Press, 2009], 7. Finally, MacKenzie Wark suggests there is a need to consider how tactical media *become tactical* and to direct more "theoretical attention to what tactical media workers are doing." MacKenzie Wark, "Strategies for Tactical Media," *RealTime* 51 [2002], available at: http://www.realtimearts.net/article/issue51/6864.

2 Gerald Vizenor, *Survivance: Narratives of Native Presence* [University of Nebraska Press, 2008], 19.

3 In the process of writing this essay, I followed the DAPL protests as they unfolded and communicated with indigenous and non-indigenous people involved in them, including drone activists Myron Dewey and Dean Dedman, Jr. I also watched many drone videos and the powerful documentary film, *Awake*, which Dewey codirected, and reviewed US documents released in FOIA requests and leaked private security firm records. I share Caren Kaplan's reticence about the idle embrace of civilian drones, sometimes called "good drones," and agree with her suggestion, building on Donna Haraway's work, that "drones are neither good or bad but always impure and hybrid." Given this, Kaplan challenges critics to always question, "who wields the weapon and for what ends?" Caren Kaplan, "Drones, Cyborgs, and the Domestic Threshold of War" [paper presented at Conference Against Drone Warfare, Duke University, October 21, 2017], 7.

4 Caren Kaplan, "Protest Drones, Citizen Journalism, and the Ambiguity of Air Space," in press, 6.

5 As Dedman puts it, "Known around camp as 'DRONE WARRIOR' I stand and fly for justice and the indigenous way of life. A drone environmental activist who exposes from the sky. I am changing the way we experience movements such as this historical gathering of so many Nations that come here to help us protect our homeland and waters from corporate greed." Dean Dedman, Jr, *Through Indigenous Eyes* [lulu.com, 2017], 70.

6 Dean Dedman Jr and Myron Dewey have both been recognized with awards for their drone media work, including an award from the 2017 New York City Documentary Film festival. For a discussion of other anti-DAPL drone interventions see Janet Walker, "Standing with Standing Rock: Media, Mapping, and Survivance," *Media Fields Journal* [June 5, 2018],

flight, environmentalism, art, and community engagement. The term Dedman uses for this amalgam is, "INDIGENOUS MEDIA," which, he insists, "HAS BEEN AROUND FOR THOUSANDS OF YEARS. WE ARE THE TRUE STORYTELLERS. IT'S IN OUR BLOOD, IN OUR HISTORY, IN OUR CHILDREN. PASSED DOWN FROM EVERY GENERATION TO THE NEXT. WE WERE HERE. WE ARE HERE. AND WE WILL CONTINUE TO EXIST IN THIS WORLD AND ONTO THE NEXT."[15]

Indeed, the indigenous media or tactical drone media of Dedman and Dewey played an integral role in shaping material conditions and knowledge about DAPL, the protestors, and the police. As these drone videos became vertical mediations, making power relations from sky to ground intelligible and palpable, their online circulation occurred through multiple commercial platforms, from Facebook to YouTube to Unicorn Riot. This meant that the ownership of drone videos often had to be surrendered to social media companies in order for them to be distributed. Thus, drone warriors were not only monitoring the theft of their lands, the compromising of their water, and protests of these actions, but, in order to share these views, had to give up their intellectual property rights to their drone videos as well. Facebook and other platforms benefitted financially from the Standing Rock protests and drone videos as some of them went viral, but Dedman and Dewey's labor went uncompensated, connecting to broader issues of immaterial labor, Indigenous American unemployment, and ownership structures within the digital economy. This predicament raises broader questions: what does it mean to live within structural conditions that allow the simultaneous theft of a sovereign nation's land, water, air, media, and digital labor? As Marisa Duarte argues in her book *Network Sovereignty,* the ownership and control of digital networks on tribal lands is a crucial issue that demands attention and action.[16]

No-Fly Zone

Despite these concerns, Indigenous Americans' drone media had serious impacts, and compelled federal and state officials to work together to impose a no-fly zone above the DAPL protest area. Between October and December 2016, North Dakota law enforcement officials communicated with Federal Aviation Administration officials in Washington, DC to request a Temporary Flight Restriction (TFR).[17] In an October 23 email to the FAA, North Dakota officials characterized the protestors as "violent" and as "organizing and deploying paramilitary style actions," which led law enforcers to intensify aerial surveillance and "provide over watch for security of the officers on the ground."[18] Ultimately, the FAA ordered a no-fly zone of almost 154 square miles from October 25 to November 4, and a smaller area was renewed twice, until December 13.

Throughout this process FAA officials coached local law enforcers on how to make a "solid case" for re-establishing the TFR. For instance, an FAA officer emphasized the need to address the "three triggering threats outlined earlier" and to get them substantiated by "federal LEAs on the ground." He

also urged the North Dakota official to insert new information about ongoing threats, and indicated in a postscript at the end of another email, a "typical scenario for our use of LE 91.137a1 TFR would be people firing at law enforcement aircraft in the area [e.g., Ferguson]," drawing a comparison between the situation in Standing Rock and the 2014 protests over the killing of Michael Brown, an unarmed black teenager, by a white police officer in Ferguson, Missouri.

In response, the North Dakota agencies expanded their rationale for the TFR renewal on four grounds: 1) the need to keep the sky clear for helicopters fighting fires; 2) a series of "near misses" between various aircraft; 3) use of high-power laser pointers and spotlights by those on the ground intended to "blind pilots overhead"; and 4) private drones flying "in a dangerous manner immediately over law enforcement officials." The request went on to claim that "UAS [or drones] have often operated at face level and have recently attempted to enter law enforcement vehicles" and have been "deliberately flown" at response aircraft and watercraft.[19]

While one FAA official recognized tribes' concerns about First Amendment infringements in his TFR correspondence, local law enforcers were ultimately more concerned about preventing their own activities from appearing in a live drone feed. As one North Dakota officer put it: "We need to ensure the movement of law enforcers trying to protect the innocent is not being broadcast live by the use of drones."[20] An email from North Dakota police to FAA reported "4–5 small UAS flying in the TFR last night harassing our law enforcement officers," and went on to identify one of the suspects, whose name was redacted, operating a UAS live feed on the indie media website, Unicorn Riot. The email message also identified the suspect's Facebook page (redacted in the FOIA release), demonstrating the state's commandeering of social media as a surveillance platform.[21]

Several key issues emerge when examining this correspondence: 1) the tight coordination between state and federal agencies in defining protestors' drone use as "violent" and "dangerous"; 2) the paternalistic claims to the vertical field as a zone of "overwatch" to protect law enforcers and "peaceful demonstrators"; 3) the inability to recognize the importance of drone video for protestors and instead to criminalize protestors' drone use and activities; and 4) the articulation of drone-based protests with other social movements deemed to be threatening to national security, such as Ferguson, Black Lives Matter, Earth First, and the American Indian Movement.

Beyond the FAA file, *The Intercept* published intelligence reports from Tiger Swan. The firm, which was gathering evidence that could be used to prosecute "persons of interest," had done security and mercenary work in Afghanistan and Iraq. In its analysis, *The Intercept* emphasizes the firm's application of military-style counterterrorism measures upon the water protectors. Tiger Swan staff not only compared protestors to jihadist fighters and terrorists, they also noted "the presence of additional Palestinians in the camp," and claimed, "the movement's involvement with Islamic individuals is a dynamic that requires further examination."[22] Ethnic and racial profiling by Tiger Swan staff was common as well, and in counterterrorism parlance, members of certain groups were referred to as "cells." This war on terror mindset was also evident in the leaked records of the so-called Intel Group as well. The group included an armada of federal officers–from the Bureau of Indian Affairs, FBI, US Marshalls, and Department of Justice– and one exchange claimed there was a "strong female Shia [Islamic] following" among the protesters.[23] The Intel Group was particularly fixated on watching live feeds via drones and social media, appropriating protestors' social media posts as intelligence data, marking the thin line between sharing and surveillance. North Dakota fusion center generated a diagram of suspects in September 2016, identifying Black Lives Matter and Anonymous connections as well.

Though drone activists were blocked from the air during the TFR, Tiger Swan and North Dakota police were allowed to continue their aerial surveillance. While a focus on the tactical aspects of drone activism can generate hope and optimism, it is also important to recognize the strategies that federal and state officials and private security workers used to remove water protectors' drones from the air, as they mobilized regulatory mechanisms, shot at them while they were in the sky, and seized them on the ground. These aggressive actions intermingled with historical tribal struggles that have played out through the vertical field–from the air to water underground– and that involve issues of eminent domain, sovereignty, and free speech.

As Dewey, and other anti-DAPL drone activists have argued, tribal claims of eminent domain extend to air space as well.[24] A basic principle of international aviation law is that a sovereign nation is entitled to "complete and exclusive sovereignty over the air space above its territory."[25] Lawyer Sandra Shippey of the Native American Practice Group in California suggests, "Tribes could assert that air traffic above tribal lands could pose a risk or threat to tribal citizens or the tribal government (especially low flying aircraft). Also, Tribes should have a right to protect its citizens from aircraft noise, air pollution, aviation accidents and other impositions from low-flying aircraft."[26] Multiple reports from DAPL protestors indicate that law enforcers' aircraft flew very low in an effort to intimidate them.

The DAPL protests are just one example of the need for further tribal assertions of sovereignty over air space. In his detailed legal analysis of this issue, lawyer and member of the Seminole tribe, William (aka John) M. Haney, argues, "tribes have an inherent sovereign right to regulate tribal airspace."[27] Beyond claims of eminent domain in the air, tribes have asserted first amendment rights through the vertical field. After Dedman flew a drone to check on the DAPL area and police shot at it, he declared, "They shot at my first amendment right. They shot at a journalist's equipment."[28] In addition to monitoring

http://mediafieldsjournal.org/standing-with-standing-rock/.

7 Some of Dean Dedman, Jr's drone videos are available here: https://www.facebook.com/pg/Drone.nation2017/videos/?ref=page_internal.

8 Personal interview of Dean Dedman, Jr via telephone, July 2018.

9 Dedman, Jr, *Through Indigenous Eyes*, 38.

10 Ibid., 55.

11 Ibid., 17.

12 Ibid., 35.

13 Description and video of this event are available on this legal fundraising website: https://fundrazr.com/91FsTe?ref=ab_4ZscoUjzPKI4ZscoUjzPKI.

14 Myron Dewey, "Standing Rock drone pilot begins jury trial next week," Creativeresistance.org, July 7, 2017, http://www.creativeresistance.org/standing-rock-drone-pilot-myron-dewey-begins-jury-trial-next-week/.

15 Dedman Jr, *Through Indigenous Eyes*, 62.

16 Marisa Elana Duarte, *Network Sovereignty: Building the Internet Across Indian Country* (University of Washington Press, 2017).

17 Samuel Waldbaum, Request for FAA Communications related to Standing Rock Temporary Flight Restriction and response to it, MuckRock, available at https://www.muckrock.com/foi/united-states-of-america-10/request-for-faa-communications-related-to-standing-rock-temporary-flight-restriction-37493/.

18 Email message, Michael Lynk (North Dakota State Radio) to Federal Aviation Authority (FAA), (October 23, 2016), ibid.

19 Email message, Sean Johnson (North Dakota Department of Emergency Services) to Rob Sweet (FAA), (November 4, 2016), ibid.

20 Email message, Sgt. Shannon Henke (North Dakota Highway Patrol) to Sean Johnson (North Dakota Department of Emergency Services), (November 4, 2016), ibid.

21 None of the FAA email messages in the MuckRock file, however, mentioned that law enforcers were using tear gas, rubber bullets, or water cannons against protestors on Nov 20 (as documented by Dewey's drone video), and that more than 300 people were injured.

22 Alleen Brown, Will Parish & Alice Speri, "Leaked Documents Reveal Counterterrorism Tactics Used at Standing Rock to Defeat 'Pipeline Insurgencies,'" *The Intercept* (May 27, 2017), https://theintercept.com/2017/05/27/leaked-documents-reveal-security-firms-counterterrorism-tactics-at-standing-rock-to-defeat-pipeline-insurgencies/; "Internal Tiger Swan Situation Report 2016-9-22," leaked to *The Intercept*, https://theintercept.com/document/2017/05/27/internal-tigerswan-situation-report-2016-09-22/.

23 "Intel Group Email Thread" (May 27, 2017), leaked to *The Intercept*, https://theintercept.com/document/2017/05/27/intel-group-email-thread.

24 Alleen Brown, Will Parish & Alice Speri, "Police Used Private Security Aircraft for Surveillance in Standing Rock No-Fly Zone" (September 29, 2017), *The Intercept*, https://theintercept.com/2017/09/29/standing-rock-dakota-access-pipeline-dapl-no-fly-zone-drones-tigerswan/.

DAPL's development, drone activists hovered above blockades and standoffs between law enforcers and protesters, trying to ensure civil rights were protected and providing oversight when they were not. As Dedman explains, "The drones provide a sense of safety to the protectors. Many have been tear gassed, pepper sprayed and shot at with rubber bullets. As the actions were going on by the water there, a lot of people told me they felt safe because there was a drone just above them watching what was going on."[29] What might have happened if live drone feeds were not running throughout the protests?

While drone use has empowered anti-DAPL protesters, it is important to recognize efforts by law enforcers, private security firms, and federal agencies (from the FAA to the FBI) to limit or thwart protesters' drone use. Doing so recognizes the vertical field as a site of power relations and ongoing social struggles. The vertical field includes air, spectrum, orbit, and ground, and has historically been claimed and colonized by state and corporate entities. One reason that tactical drone videos have been so powerful is that they challenged the vertical hegemony of the state, which sought to control everything from the sky to the electromagnetic spectrum to the water and oil underground. In the process, representatives of these groups restricted protesters' air access, damaged and confiscated drone pilots' equipment, intimidated and spied on protesters, and compromised breathable air using pepper spray, tear gas, and water cannons. While the standoff between protesters and law enforcers often manifest visually as scenes of militarized equipment on one end and protesters holding hands on the other, it also unfolded through the vertical field as a battle between civilian drones and police airplanes and helicopters, between those protecting water and those protecting oil. In this way, we can understand the DAPL protests as generating practices of vertical mediation – what happened in the air above Standing Rock directly affected bodies, material relations, and lifeworlds on and under the ground. It altered where and how people moved, what sites they sought to protect, and what technologies and practices they used to do so.

25 William M. Haney, *Protecting Tribal Skies: Why Indian Tribes Possess the Sovereign Authority to Regulate Tribal Airspace*, 40 AM. INDIAN L. REV. 1 (2016), https://digitalcommons.law.ou.edu/ailr/vol40/iss1/1, 3.

26 Sandra L. Shippey, "What's Up? Native American Aviation and Air Space," *Procopio: Legal Counsel to Tribal Governments and Business* (November 11, 2016), https://bloggingcircle.wordpress.com/2016/11/11/whats-up-native-american-aviation-and-airspace/.

27 William M. Haney, *Protecting Tribal Skies*, 6.

28 "Police Shooting Down Aerial Drone" video from The Real News Network, embedded in Larae Meadows, "FAA Complicity in Violence against Standing Rock Water Protectors – Part 2," https://nativenewsonline.net/currents/faa-complicity-violence-standing-rock-water-protectors-part-2/.

29 Dedman, Jr, *Through Indigenous Eyes*, 77.

Opposite: Stills from drone footage of protestor/police confrontations.

Acknowledgments

The author would like to thank Dr Adrienne Keene for inviting her to participate in the Siouxveillance Forum at Brown University in April 2018, and inspiring her to write about this topic. The author would also like to thank Myron Dewey and Dean Dedman, Jr for sharing their insights and experiences.

OF PITS AND PADS

JEFFREY S. NESBIT + DAVID SALOMON

Jeffrey S. Nesbit is an architect, urbanist, and doctoral candidate at Harvard Graduate School of Design. His research focuses on urbanism, infrastructure, and the evolution of technical lands. Nesbit is currently writing an architectural history of the 20th-century US spaceport complex and is co-editor of *Chasing the City* (2018) and *New Geographies 11: Extraterrestrial* (2019).

David Salomon is an assistant professor of art history and the coordinator of architectural studies at Ithaca College, and a lecturer at The University of Pennsylvania's Weitzman School of Design. He is author of *Symmetry: The One and the Many* (2018), co-author of *The Architecture of Patterns* (2010), and co-curator of the traveling exhibition *Ambiguous Territory: Architecture, Landscape, and the Postnatural*. He is currently researching the architecture and landscapes of astronomical and meteorological observatories.

✚ MILITARY SCIENCES, TECHNOLOGY, DESIGN

Understanding the behaviors and potentials of the Earth's surface is increasingly dependent on capturing its energy and transforming it into images. Using a variety of technologies, including telemetric data signaled from low-Earth orbit satellites, Earth's surface is constantly being monitored and manipulated. Our ability to know, imagine, and occupy the geological realm is dependent upon our capacity to deploy certain technologies in the celestial one.[2] One place where these two realms intersect is in space launch complexes. The locations and designs of these sites have their own geographical and geopolitical histories, which provide a unique perspective on the ideological and aesthetic relationships that increasingly tether the terrestrial to extraterrestrial territories.

Historically, space launch complexes are firmly anchored to the terrestrial surface. No longer. Rockets can now be deployed and retrieved from water-based platforms. What significance, if any, might this movement from land to sea suggest? In looking at the forms and history of launch sites, with specific emphasis on their relationship to the ground, their aesthetic, and their connection to other systems, this essay looks at how the design of these complexes reveals the changing relationship between ourselves and the Earth. This critical lens briefly surveys a cross-section of space history: from the World War II experiments of the German military with ballistic missiles, to the open pits of the Soviets' space program, to the concrete pads of the Americans' Saturn Rockets, to the emergence of

the private space company SpaceX's and China's new ocean-borne platforms. These launch complex sites represent and help produce the transformation of the Earth from a thick solid object to a networked information-rich surface. As this shift occurs, the literal ground becomes less important (and more at risk) and the web for technologically monitoring it becomes more and more robust.

Pits

In 1936—five years before the United States military built its historic test sites at Los Alamos, New Mexico—the German military began to test ballistic missiles at an "ultra-secret facility" known as Peenemunde. Located along the northwestern German coastline, the site was designed by Albert Speer, the well-known German architect who worked on many of Germany's political and military projects during World War II. As described by Jean-Louis Cohen, the project was organized in accordance with "the principles of traditional town planning" with its "axial plan" creating a direct connection between its associated housing complex and a "railway station with a monumental entrance."[3] The rocket launch portion of the complex was enclosed by a sloped-earth embankment with a truncated pyramidal section and an elliptically shaped plan that helped contain the blast emitted by the missiles. The result is a massive artificial pit. In short, it had a monumental, if not an ancient sensibility consistent with Speer's other work and his political position in the Nazi party.

Peenemunde's highly geometric layout included test towers, a flame trench, and underground rooms that housed a control room with switchboards. Foreshadowing the soon to be normative relationship at launch sites between an invisible infrastructural network and a pronounced landscape, the testing facilities were organized by a dense series of mechanical conduit lines connecting it to the rest of the complex by long underground corridors. Such lines produced an early indication of network applying and managing technology. Not

so different from William Mitchell's description of a "networked cognitive system" from "spatial and material embodiment," the launch complex merged communication operations with a reconfigured ground.[4]

This arrangement was part of a trend. Traditionally, the military operated only on the surface of Earth. Not until the 19th century do we find an expansion of the ground through the flights of new machines and the carving down into buried networks of communication. Modern military infrastructure was thus thickened into a three-dimensional map, with each zone producing a stratification of organizational networks. The move underground came with its own sensibilities and associations. It was less organized and less formal than what one found on the surface. Through the "blending of human artifacts in the landscape" with subterranean technologies, the launch complex created an "artificial division of a shared landscape," one that simultaneously contained imperceptible automated systems and the imaginary perspective of space exploration.[5]

Whereas the Germans literally built-up the earth to create their elliptical launch zone, the Soviet space program dug right into it. The Baikonur Cosmodrome, located in present day Kazakhstan, is where Sputnik set off into space. It was the first (April 12, 1961) and the most recent (July 20, 2019) manned space flight. Yuri Gagarin was launched into space from Site #1, which was quickly nicknamed "Gagarin's Start." With the launch complex still in use today, its design has hardly changed. From an aerial perspective the site appears as a strip mine with a generic concrete structure anchoring one leg of the triangular pit. This exposed hole in the ground serves as the flame trench that captures and deflects the boosters' exhaust away from the rocket on the pad.

The site was chosen, in part, because it is flat. The seemingly empty landscape allowed for uninterrupted "radio-visible" space between the triangulated radio-controlled navigation

1936

● V2 Missile

PEENEMUNDE :
Germany

system that was comprised of two stations oriented on either side of the pad. This system was an offshoot of the vast network of monitoring equipment used for tracking and guiding ballistic missiles – a network that would grow more geographically and technologically robust as the Soviet space program expanded. All information was sent back to the ground station at Baikonur.[6] Five years later, the radio-monitoring of the launch itself would be rendered obsolete by an internal navigation system, thus rendering the space required for the previous arrangement unnecessary. However, the amount of resources already dedicated to Baikonur sealed its fate as the permanent home of Soviet space travel.[7]

While the launch complex pit has a literal connection with the Earth, the rocket itself never touches it. Soviet rockets were built horizontally and transported to the pad via rail. There they were propped upright against the structural service towers. The contrast between the smooth metal rocket and the rough earthen pit at Gagarin's Start illustrates the historian of science and technology Rosalind Williams's point that even though it may not look designed "the subterranean environment is a technological one"; it is an environment that exists within an ideological map that combines machines, imagination, and places.[8] The barrenness of the desert, the rawness of the pit, and the hyper-technological image of the rockets at Baikonur respectively embody three distinct modes of the sublime—the vast, the defiled, and the technological—each one representing the violent power required to simultaneously transform the Earth's surface and to leave its gravitational pull.

Pads

The development of the Kennedy Space Center (formerly known as Launch Operations Center), and particularly Launch Pad 39A, was indebted to German precedents and personalities. Peenemunde's launch pad complex and associated network of systems directly impacted the designs for the new military launch complex on Merritt Island in Florida. This was due, in part, because these efforts were led by German emigres and leaders in rocket science and development Werner von Braun and Kurt Debus. By April of 1961, a decision was reached to modify earlier military launch complexes into a state-of-the-art "mobile launch concept" – substantially changing functions, distances, and facility requirements for sending rockets into space. The choice of Cape Canaveral along the central coast of Florida was made because of the site's remoteness for security, and proximity to the equator for better alignment with Earth's orbit. To accommodate new technologies for the Saturn V rocket, the complex was scheduled to include four launch pads (only two were constructed), a mobile transporter to move rockets vertically from an assembly building, a path connecting assembly and launch, and a launch control facility.

Along with other necessary infrastructure—such as a large turning basin, fuel storage, and underground tunnels—the new mobile launch concept required a massive integration of multiple systems, including an extensive reconfiguration of ground. In 1962, NASA began dredging hydraulic fill from the Banana River, pumping silt into the construction site to raise the pads out of sea level. The government also initiated massive wharf construction with a series of barge canals and turning basins. Two large pyramid-like sand piles were constructed to elevate the launch pads used to send the Saturn V rocket to the Moon. These were subsequently covered in concrete. This building-up of an artificial ground echoes the engineered topography at Peenemunde. So too does the faceted geometry of the concrete pad itself, and the flame trench underneath it. The network of groundwork at Launch Complex 39—from the paved roads to the water channels, and especially the pads themselves—became completely synthesized as mechanized ground.

The earthmoving and surface-covering practices used at the Kennedy Space Center literally leave us with a stratified ground, a fragmented history, and a geopolitical territory that was leveled, re-leveled, and soon abandoned. It is a technological

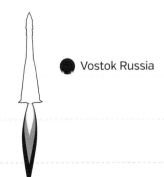

● Vostok Russia

GAGARIN'S START :
Soviet Union

world, one in which human inventions supersede natural environments. Earthmoving practices in the spaceport complex illustrate a world in which both real *and* imaginary narratives about the function of the ground are presented as structurally congruent. The reconfigured and subsequently encased ground of the pad site represents a place of extreme displacement from the natural environment—a new, completely manufactured world; a world with a refined sensibility of consistently smooth surfaces designed for the departure from Earth.

Launch Pad 39A was linked to other infrastructural networks near and far. Rocket parts were sent directly to the site from the NASA Michoud Assembly Facility in New Orleans by barge. Communications lines routed information from the launch pad to the Launch Control Center three miles away and onto the Johnson Space Center in Houston. While Rosalind Williams recognizes that "unlike the mine, the spaceship fails to convey a sense of permanent enclosure in a finite world," the launch pad itself is such a world.[9] At the launch pad site, the dialectic between an infinite world of movement (technology) and a finite world of stasis (ground) is synthesized and manipulated. But it's a world, it is a ground, albeit an artificial one. However, unlike the iconic rockets and similarly photogenic launch towers, the pads have little place in the public's imaginary of the space program. A closer look reveals that their locally symmetrical shapes and their smooth, sloping surfaces (used to elevate the pads above sea level and to accommodate the crawler) are quite elegant; except at liftoff— when filled with fire, sound, and water—there is a surprising serenity about them.

Perhaps nowhere is the combination of stasis and movement, of a resistant Earth and transformative technologies, better witnessed than the Missile Crawler Transporter. It was used as a vehicle for slowly transporting rockets along the three-mile-long paved surface from the Vertical Assembly Building to the elevated Launch Complex 39 pads. The crawler was derived from the steam-shovel crawler used for surface mining, primarily for coal in Kentucky.

What began as a machine to manipulate and extract energy from the Earth was translated and transformed into a device that assisted our departure from it.

Proliferation

The geometrical configuration of Launch Pad 39A was quickly modified to accommodate the Space Shuttle program. And again, in early 2011, the pad was changed to house the SpaceX rocket program. The ground was manipulated, the pad made slimmer, and the size of its top surface was reduced for the smaller rockets it now supports. However, it maintains its faceted, symmetrical profile, and calm presence.

The fate of 39A is unusual. Of the 36 launch complexes built in the Cape Canaveral wetlands, only two remain operational. The others lie in different degrees of ruin, none will likely be reused, nor will they return to their natural landscape. In contrast to this consolidation, the number of launch sites around the world has increased. From the original two (Baikonur and Cape Canaveral) there have been 31 sites sending objects into space, with 21 of them still in operation.

In recent years the number of launches from these locations has also exploded. From 1964 to 2012 there was a steady average of 130 launches per year. Since then it has jumped to 288 per year. These are almost exclusively for positioning satellites in low orbit. Currently there are 4,987 satellites orbiting the Earth, though only about 1,900 (or 40%) of them are operational based on numbers published by the United Nations Office for Outer Space.[10] And yet, according to the Union of Concerned Scientists, the satellites currently orbiting the Earth are broken down into distinct types including: 777 communications satellites, 710 Earth observation satellites, 223 technology development and demonstration satellites, 137 navigation and positioning satellites, 85 space science and observation satellites, and 25 satellites for Earth science activities.[11]

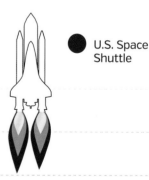

U.S. Space Shuttle

From a single site in Germany, a single complex in the Soviet Union, and a network of 36 pads in Florida, we now have an interconnected system with thousands of satellites, hundreds of operation centers and labs, and dozens of launch sites. Currently there are over 20 active launch spaceports worldwide. Each of these space centers may include over a dozen launch pads. The importance of a few places has given way to a scientific-economic-military network where the location and origin of any one site is less important than its ability to link with another node in the system. Within this network, space is less explored than it is being colonized in order to more closely examine and exploit the Earth's surface. The more of that thick surface (which includes the "critical zone" of the atmosphere and the small substrata where life takes hold) we are able to monitor, the less important any one piece of it becomes.[12]

Platforms

On June 5, 2019, the Chinese space industry sent a Long March 11 solid propellant rocket into space from a "mobile launch platform" in the Yellow Sea.[13] The payload included two satellites that will monitor Earth's atmospheric and surface behaviors along with five communications satellites.[14] Though it was the first ocean-based launch since the private Sea Launch service was suspended in 2014, it appears to be the beginning of a new era of such services by China's Academy of Launch Vehicle Technology.

The launch platform used by China's Academy of Launch Vehicle Technology is a flat barge in the ocean with two small towers flanking the 68.25-foot-tall rocket. Its sensibility is infrastructural. It looks like a small container ship or oil rig. It is minimalist rather than monumental. This is a far cry from the design of previous rocket launch sites, which were both massive and required much earth to be moved.

Among the advantages of this portable, sea-based system is the ability to deploy rockets closer to the equator, where the faster rotational speed of the Earth makes it possible to escape

1 Marshall McLuhan, "The Invisible Environment: The Future of an Erosion," *Perspecta* 11 (1967): 166.

2 John J. May, "Sensing: Preliminary Notes on the Emergence of Statistical-Mechanical Geographic Vision," *Perspecta* 40 (2008): 42–53.

3 Jean-Louis Cohen, *Architecture in Uniform: Designing and Building for the Second World War* (Yale University Press and Canadian Centre for Architecture, 2011), 295–99.

4 William J. Mitchell, *Me++: The Cyborg Self and the Networked City* (MIT Press, 2003), 19.

5 See Alessandra Ponte, "Desert Testing," in Antoine Picon & Alessandra Ponte (eds), *Architecture and the Sciences: Exchanging Metaphors* (Princeton Architectural Press, 2003), 80–82.

6 Christian Lardier & Stefan Barensky, *The Soyuz Launch Vehicle: The Two Lives of an Engineering Triumph* (Springer, 2013), 40. See also, RussianSpaceWeb.com, "Centers: Ground Control Stations," (accessed on July 22, 2019).

7 Vladimir Suvorov & Alexander Sabelnikov, *The First Manned Spaceflight: Russia's Quest for Space* (Nova, 1997).

8 Rosalind Williams, *Notes on the Underground: An Essay on Technology, Society, and the Imagination* (MIT Press, 2008), 7.

9 Ibid., 7.

10 Numbers are generated by the United Nations Office for Outer Space Affairs (UNOOSA), and the Union of Concerned Scientists. See "How Many Satellites Orbiting the Earth in 2019" in *Analytics*, https://www.pixalytics.com/satellites-orbiting-earth-2019/.

11 The Union of Concerned Scientists collected "in-depth details on the 2,062 satellites currently orbiting Earth," Union of Concerned Scientists, "UCS Satellite Database," https://www.ucsusa.org/nuclear-weapons/space-weapons/satellite-database (accessed on July 22, 2019).

12 See more on Latour's description of a "critical zone" in Bruno Latour, *Down to Earth: Politics in the New Climatic Regime* (Polity Press, 2018), 82–99.

13 See Charles Benson & William B. Faherty, *Moonport: A History of Apollo Launch Facilities and Operations* (NASA, 1978). In the early 1960s as rockets transitioned from the military to NASA's efforts to launch to the Moon, the spaceport was redesigned as a "mobile launch complex," under the leadership of Kurt Debus. Curiously, the continued reliance on "mobile launch" remains decades later with new rising leaders of space travel in the Asian continent.

its gravitational force with less fuel.[15] This strategy also has the advantage of having lower infrastructural costs and being more covert – qualities that are attractive to both the business and military communities. It also provides the ability to "hit any orbit without being constrained to a set geographic area."[16] In short, the mobile launch expanded to a sea-based approach seems to render the Earth's geography, or at least its land mass, obsolete.

Until recently, the leap into outer-space was associated with a unique spot on the Earth's surface. This specific ground is what Bruno Latour refers to as "Terrestrial" space.[17] He defines it as distinct from "Global" space in that the latter is an abstract notion, independent of the literal stuff of the planet. It is a network without things. Global space is invisible and empty even though, or precisely because, it is constantly observed and monitored, whereas Terrestrial space is always occupied.

The shift of the launch sites to the sea reinforces the fact that our technologies (and our culture) require groundlessness. It is more and more Global. We no longer need to manipulate or occupy the Terrestrial in order to live in or leave it. There are no launch sites per se, no more networks to bury belowground, or earth to be moved when the entire ocean is an infinitely large launch site. When everything is a network, everything is hidden – in the ocean, in outer space, and in the clouds. This invisibility is echoed in the sensibility of the launch and landing platforms used by China and SpaceX. Far from iconic, they instead aspire to disappear. Or, in Marshall McLuhan's terms, they aspire to be a part of an always invisible "total and saturating environment."[18] If there is nothing to see everything is difficult to imagine.

The Earth Obsolete

In 1967, McLuhan noticed the Earth-as-environment was no longer in the background. The environment, and Earth itself, was becoming a highly visible and malleable "art form." This new situation, he maintained, was a direct result of the planet being probed by a network of "satellites and electronic antennae."[19] The subsequent rise of "environmental consciousness" gave rise to an increase of "environmental science" through the military apparatus. The military as a scientific organization, began "setting up bases in remote areas" to measure and monitor the globe.[20] And, as the Cold War dissolved, "scientists could continue to keep the Earth under perpetual surveillance, with help from the relics of the Cold War" such as spy satellites.[21]

The production and use of technologies for extraterrestrial space are deep reflections of culture, politics, and life on Earth. But, as McLuhan recognized, what is more pressing than what is envisioned by these machines is how perception and the image of the world has changed.[22] What had been the physical context for life was now a supplier of cultural content, of matter and data. As Bruno Latour notes, the environment is both a product of human inhabitation and a representation of the human to nature relationship. It is both a real and an imagined duality. If the "natural world and the susceptibility of humans to dangers on an enormous scale" were recognized as sublime in the Cold War era, the scale of the present dangers posed by our treatment of Earth has proven to be more difficult to represent.[23] Global warming does not yet have an icon equivalent to the nuclear age's mushroom cloud or the space age's rocket launch.

Of course, neither these two images, nor the devices that generated them have gone away. And yet, these technologies for extraterrestrial space and tools of geopolitical power have become a part of our saturated, technologized environment. Where spectacle was, the conventional shall be.

Rocket launch sites and satellites with their network of "electronic antennas" also persist.[24] As indicated above, their numbers have dramatically increased. But, as the evolution of launch pads and recovery sites illustrate, they are less dependent on terrestrial space, more remote, and out of sight. This not only suggests the terrestrial territory of Earth has expanded to include its entire surface; the Earth's surface is increasingly imagined less as a Buckminster Fuller spaceship and environment to live in, and more as a technology to be made use of.[25] While it is true that SpaceX rockets still take off from the *terra firma* of Launch Pad 39A, their rocket boosters land on a barge in the ocean to be recycled for the next launch. And lest we forget, the stated goal of the company is to abandon Earth for Mars. As such, it both imagines and works to create a time when the Earth—its ground, its water, and its air—is just another obsolete technology.

SpaceX
Falcon 9

14 Not unlike the reclamation of an older technological piece of equipment for mining the Earth, the Sea Launch platform was a retrofitted mobile oil drilling platform, see Andrew Jones, "China Gains New Flexible Launch Capabilities with First Sea Launch," *Spacenews* (June 19, 2019), https://spacenews.com/china-gains-new-flexible-launch-capabilities-with-first-sea-launch/.

15 The mobile launch platform used in the June 5 launch is owned and run by a Chinese maritime engineering company, which wished not to be named in the press due to contractual obligations. See Zhae Lei, "China's First Seaborne Rocket Launched in Yellow Sea," *The Telegraph* (June 19, 2019), https://www.telegraph.co.uk/china-watch/technology/seaborne-rocket-launched-in-yellow-sea/.

16 See Jones, "China Gains..."

17 Latour, *Down to Earth*.

18 McLuhan, "The Invisible Environment," 164.

19 Ibid., 165.

20 Jacob Hamblin, *Arming Mother Nature: The Birth of Catastrophic Environment* (Oxford University Press, 2013), 90.

21 See Lisa Parks, *Down to Earth: Satellite Technologies, Industries and Cultures* (Rutgers University Press, 2012).

22 See William Rankin, *After the Map: Cartography, Navigation, and the Transformation of Territory in the Twentieth Century* (University of Chicago Press, 2016), 19–20. From the position of mapping, Rankin suggests that we should not focus on the powerfulness of the military, but rather understand how we, as designers, can "participate in new geographies and new forms of territorial power," considering that territory can constantly mutate and network.

23 Hamblin, *Arming Mother Nature*, 251. Hamblin claims the arms race produced from satellites and ICBMs generated a cultural change in how "the world seems smaller and made the most far-fetched visions of the future seem possible...Scientists working with the military extended 'total war' thinking to the natural environment, to maximize the catastrophic consequences of war. In the process, they fostered a profound belief in the manipulability of the natural world and the susceptibility of humans to dangers on an enormous scale."

24 Rankin, *After the Map*, 15.

25 See Buckminster Fuller, *Operating Manual for Spaceship Earth* (Simon and Schuster, 1969).

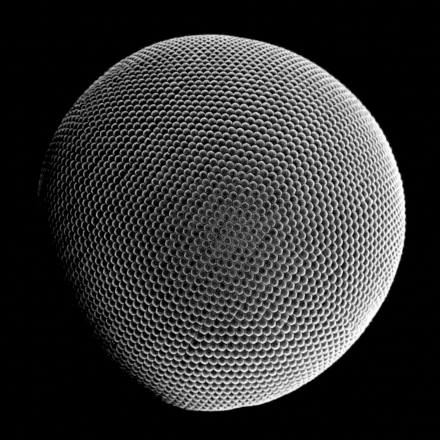

DOUGLAS ROBB + KAREN BAKKER
PLANETARY VOYEURISM

Douglas Robb is a PhD candidate, Four Year Fellow, and Vanier Doctoral Scholar in the Department of Geography at the University of British Columbia. He is also an instructor at UBC's School of Architecture + Landscape Architecture. Doug's research explores the intersection of design, political ecology, and political economy in extractive landscapes. He holds a master's degree in landscape architecture from the University of Toronto, for which he received the Canadian Society of Landscape Architects' Award of Merit.

Karen Bakker is professor, Canada Research Chair, and director of the Program on Water Governance at the University of British Columbia. She was awarded her PhD in 1999 from the School of Geography and Environment at Oxford University, where she studied as a Rhodes Scholar. Karen is a member of the Board of the International Institute for Sustainable Development, and the Scientific Advisory Committee of the Council of Canadian Academies. She is a Pierre Elliott Trudeau Foundation Fellow and a member of the Royal Society of Canada's College of New Scholars, Artists and Scientists. She was named one of Canada's Top 40 under 40 in 2011.

✚ GEOGRAPHY, CARTOGRAPHY

Opposite: Compound eye of Antarctic krill.

At the back of the d'Harnoncourt Gallery in the Philadelphia Museum of Art, visitors will find a dim hallway sealed shut by a plaster wall. In the center of the wall is a pair of antique wooden doors ringed with brick. But the doors are locked, and there is no obvious way to open them. Confused, some visitors will turn away and resume browsing the gallery. But a careful observer might notice two small holes drilled at eye-level through the center of the doorway. The wood around the holes is worn smooth, presumably by the foreheads of countless previous visitors who have peered through. Everything about the scene entices the curious visitor to take a look: the odd dead-end hallway, the old wooden doors, and the mystery of what lies beyond them. The visitor might feel apprehensive about touching the doors and violating gallery etiquette, but their curiosity is piqued. After a furtive glance behind their shoulder to make sure no one is watching, the visitor brings their face to the door and peeks through.

Through the peepholes, the visitor sees a stone wall smashed open to reveal the nude body of a woman lying in a thicket. Her face is hidden by a lock of blonde hair, but her pale and oddly malformed body is otherwise exposed. In her left hand, she holds up a small gas lamp that emits a faint orange glow. Behind the woman there is a waterfall that flows into a small pool set within a forested landscape. Despite signs of apparent trauma, the scene is eerily calm. Alarmed, the visitor pulls their face away from the door, unsure about what they have just seen. Is the tableau transgressive, or the scene of a crime? After the initial shock has passed the visitor might choose to walk away, but perhaps their desire to know more will persuade them to take a second look. It is in this moment that their desire to look changes from innocent curiosity to incipient voyeurism. Called to bear witness to a catastrophe behind a mysterious door, but unable to participate or intervene, the visitor must satisfy their desires through observation alone.

These paragraphs describe an encounter with Marcel Duchamp's artwork entitled *Étant donnés: 1° la chute d'eau, 2° le gaz d'éclairage...* (in English: *Given: 1. The Waterfall, 2. The Illuminating Gas*).[1] Duchamp's work has been widely discussed and critiqued from a variety of perspectives, including important feminist critiques that expose the work as an apparatus of the male gaze.[2] *Étant donnés* beckons us to behold the scene of a catastrophe, and in turn transforms our curiosity to know into a voyeuristic desire to watch. The scene, of course, is completely artificial: Duchamp skillfully manipulates light, shadow, and foreshortening to fabricate a tableau that feels disturbingly realistic. Yet we do not realize (or care) that the myopic view provided by the doorway disguises a trompe-l'œil: the peepholes conveniently facilitate observation, and this partial view satisfies our need to look, transforming the viewer into a spectator.

In revisiting Duchamp's artwork, our intention is to develop an analogy for contemporary methods of depicting the Anthropocene. We are particularly concerned with the methods and techniques used by geographers and landscape architects; specifically, the smooth digital spaces of geospatial data and computational representation. We coin the term "planetary voyeurism" to describe the (unintended) consequences of abstract visualizations of environmental impacts. In our analogy, the large and small catastrophes of the Anthropocene are represented by Duchamp's tableau, digital technologies of global environmental perception are represented by the doorway and its peepholes, and we (geographers, landscape architects, and others engaged in the visualization of Earth) are the voyeurs.

Why do we invoke this analogy? Because, we argue, it reveals something important about environmental visualizations that have now become ubiquitous and increasingly powerful. Over the past decade, innovative digital technologies such as satellites, drones, and distributed environmental sensing networks, combined with ever-cheaper cloud-based computing, have enabled geographers and designers to "see" environmental changes on a planetary scale. An unprecedented amount of geodata is now available, at rapidly decreasing cost.[3] These data have enabled a broad range of innovative visualization techniques to represent complex patterns of human impact upon Earth.

Those developing these visualizations are often well-intentioned, seeking to draw attention to the catastrophic effects of the Anthropocene. But when we visualize Earth, which perspectives do we privilege, and what perceptions and actions do these visualizations enable? Global environmental change trends– such as unchecked carbon emissions or biodiversity loss–have become focal points for architects and landscape architects who desire to represent and intervene in processes of ecological degradation.[4] In this paper, we query the visualizations that are mobilized in response to that desire. We caution that technologically mediated ways of seeing and perceiving global environmental change, while certainly valuable and informative, often arise from and/or produce an (unintended) voyeurism. We offer the concept of planetary voyeurism in order to spark a dialogue about how visual practices of abstraction and aestheticization might obscure the intimate and variegated dimensions of the Anthropocene.

Where might planetary voyeurism be encountered? We observe this concept in recent trends in landscape architectural discourse. For example: planetary urbanism and its predilection for top-down, orthographic visualizations that imply a comprehensive global perspicacity.[5] We also notice similar trends in landscape urbanism, ecological urbanism, landscape infrastructure, and cognate fields, including our own field of geography.[6] Across these disciplines, scholars and practitioners utilize visualizations of complex socioecological relationships to guide the analysis, planning, design, and, albeit more rarely, (re)construction of eco-technical environments. The implicit purpose of these visualizations is to translate our contemporary moment of crisis (i.e., the Anthropocene) into a site for action: "something we must take responsibility for, something we can design."[7]

The images produced through planetary voyeurism are simultaneously beautiful, abstract, and authoritative. They convey an impression of omniscience and technocratic expertise that can be leveraged to legitimize designed interventions in a landscape. Zeynep Çelik Alexander broadly characterizes these developments as "neo-naturalism," in which the traditional sources of design inspiration have been replaced by a new evidentiary regime grounded in quantitative data.[8] We build upon Alexander's argument to suggest that digital visual technologies not only provide a new lexicon for designers and geographers, but also actively interpellate viewers as passive witnesses to catastrophe. Planetary voyeurism implicates the viewer in "wanting" (and hence "reinforcing") the Anthropocene as a primarily human creation, as well as a knowable and therefore controllable condition.

This is not an entirely new phenomenon. The material and discursive power of environmental visualizations is a longstanding focus of critical geographic inquiry (consider, for example, the role of cartography in rendering landscapes legible to colonization, regulation, and/or resource extraction).[9] However, the ubiquity of innovative digital technologies coupled with the existential threats posed by climate change appears to have produced a new and urgent impulse to visualize in order to exert control. We suggest that this impulse derives from a voyeuristic desire to find and observe the messy spaces of environmental catastrophe so as to render such spaces technical and sanitized.[10] Through our efforts to visualize and ameliorate the effects of the Anthropocene, geographers and designers risk committing a secondary act of violence by erasing the multiple dimensions of knowledge and identity that cannot be captured through digital data alone. The absence of relationality in these visual abstractions recalls the masculinist gaze of Duchamp's artwork. Planetary voyeurism purports to illuminate our present condition, but there is much that it also obscures.

Art historian Irmgard Emmelhainz argues that Anthropocene does not inaugurate a new image of the world, but rather "a radical change in the conditions of visuality."[11] To illustrate this point, we situate contemporary digital visual technologies within a broad historical arc of militarized sight. Many of the technologies now common in geography and design (such as GIS and remote sensing) originated within the military as a way to perceive and support interventions in an enemy territory. These technologies have long since migrated to civilian applications, but their social and cultural resonance as tools of surveillance, discipline, and control continue to exert a powerful influence.[12] For example, aerial drones designed for combat operations have been repurposed to conduct landscape surveillance for environmental conservation.[13] Automated (or semi-automated) drones can easily outpace the speed and territorial coverage of a human on foot, and provide a wealth of geodata for designers and cartographers. However, as geographer Derek Gregory has demonstrated, the use of drone technology for landscape surveillance reconstitutes environmental conservation under a scopic regime of militarized sight.[14] Multispectral data collected by the drone provides an "objective" basis for interventions in a landscape, while multispecies relations on the ground are rendered invisible by the drone's limited perceptual capabilities (to say nothing of the heterogeneous ontologies that also exist on the land).[15] But who empowers digital information as the basis for designed interventions in the material world? How are our attempts to mitigate the effects of the Anthropocene conditioned by our technologically-mediated perceptions?

We can observe how planetary voyeurism operates in architecture and landscape architecture through visual techniques of resilient design. The concept of resilience has emerged as a prominent discourse through which the acute effects of the Anthropocene can be triaged through landscape interventions, such as green infrastructures.[16] Just as the threat of attack is used to justify military action, resilience requires the presence of an imminent but unrealized catastrophe in order to legitimize preventative interventions in a landscape. And so we turn to digital visual technologies to find and identify these threats (biodiversity loss, sea level rise, deforestation, etc.) in order to stage our tactical interventions (be it a designed landscape, an infrastructure, or a research article). This is not to suggest that the threats themselves are not real. However, we argue that digital visual technologies transform how we see and relate to the world around us, enabling yet simultaneously constraining our ability to perceive ecological relationships, and imagine alternative political and material worlds. Hence, we query the desire to visualize the Anthropocene as a pervasive and imminent threat without also interrogating the "actors, objects, practices, discourses and affects that entrain the people who are made part of it and constitute them as particular kinds of subjects."[17]

We do not mean to suggest that the solution to planetary voyeurism is simply to power down our digital devices, or reject technologically mediated modes of perception in favor of a romantic return-to-nature. Moreover, we recognize that by framing planetary voyeurism through an analogy to Duchamp's *Étant donnés*, we risk being misinterpreted as invoking a binary between experience and representation of the natural world. It might be possible to misread our critique of planetary voyeurism as a rejection of digital visual technologies. However, we do not seek to tacitly uphold a false binary between visual representation and embodied experiences of nature. Rather, our intention is to advocate for modes of multi-sensorial representation that transcend the representation/experience binary. In other words, we want to dismantle Duchamp's door.

What do we mean by "multi-sensorial" modes of representation? Imagine walking through a forest. Recall the feeling of dappled light on your skin, and the fresh smell of leaves and buds unfurling in the sun. What produces that scent? Terpenes. Trees are nature's master perfumers, and each tree produces a

1 Marcel Duchamp, "Étant donnés: 1° la chute d'eau, 2° le gaz d'éclairage...," Mixed media assemblage, 1946–1966, Philadelphia Museum of Art.

2 Amelia Jones, *Postmodernism and the En-Gendering of Marcel Duchamp* (Cambridge University Press, 1994); Julian H. Haladyn, "A Contribution to the Study of the Fantasies of Sexual Perversion in Marcel Duchamp's *Étant Donnés*," *International Journal of Žižek Studies* 7, no. 2 (2016): 1–11; Elvan Zabunyan, "Striptease: Désarticuler Duchamp par le Genre," *Cahiers Philosophiques* 131, no. 4 (2012): 64–82.

3 William Adams, "Geographies of Conservation II: Technology, Surveillance and Conservation by Algorithm," *Progress in Human Geography* 43, no. 2 (2019): 337–50; James Adams, Rob Kitchin & Agnieszka Leszczyński, "Digital Turn, Digital Geographies?" *Progress in Human Geography* 42, no. 1 (2018): 25–43; Bradley Cantrell & Justine Holzman, *Responsive Landscapes: Strategies for Responsive Technologies in Landscape Architecture* (Routledge, 2016); Jennifer Gabrys, *Program Earth: Environmental Sensing Technology and the Making of a Computational Planet* (University of Minnesota Press, 2016).

4 Greet De Block, "Ecological Infrastructure in a Critical-Historical Perspective: From Engineering 'Social' Territory to Encoding 'Natural' Topography," *Environment and Planning A* 48, no. 2 (2016): 367–90.

5 Neil Brenner, *Implosions/Explosions* (Jovis, 2014).

6 Charles Waldheim, *Landscape as Urbanism: A General Theory* (Princeton University Press, 2016); Mohsen Mostafavi & Gareth Doherty (eds), *Ecological Urbanism* (Lars Müller Publishers, 2016); Pierre Bélanger, "Landscape as Infrastructure," *Landscape Journal* 28, no. 1 (2009): 79–95.

7 Richard Weller, "Has Landscape Architecture Failed?" *The Dirt* (July 19, 2019), https://dirt.asla.org/2016/03/23/has-landscape-architecture-failed/.

8 Zeynep Çelik Alexander, "Neo-Naturalism," *Log* 31 (2014): 24.

9 Denis Cosgrove, Geography and Vision: *Seeing, Imagining and Representing the World* (I.B. Tauris, 2012).

10 Tania Murray Li, *The Will to Improve: Governmentality, Development, and the Practice of Politics* (Duke University Press, 2007); Paul Robbins & Sarah A. Moore, "Ecological Anxiety Disorder: Diagnosing the Politics of the Anthropocene," *Cultural Geographies* 20, no. 1 (2013): 3–19.

11 Irmgard Emmelhainz, "Neoliberalism, Modernity and Panic of Entropy: Undoing the Knot of the Anthropocene?" *Jeu de Paume* (December 12, 2018), http://lemagazine.jeudepaume.org/blogs/irmgard-emmelhainz/en/2018/12/14/neoliberalism-modernity-and-panic-of-entropy-undoing-the-knot-of-the-anthropocene/.

12 Torin Monahan, "Ways of Being Seen: Surveillance Art and the Interpellation of Viewing Subjects," *Cultural Studies* 32, no. 4 (2018): 561.

unique mix of terpenes—a class of volatile organic compounds—which act like signals. Trees use terpenes to fulfill a variety of needs: to summon insect bodyguards to fend off predators, to control air temperature (some terpenes can seed clouds and cool the forest), attract pollinators, fight infections, and even warn neighboring trees of pest invasions. Each tree acts as its own pharmacy, dispensing medicine as needed.[18] Terpenes are not only useful for trees, they are also valuable for humans. When we walk through a forest and inhale terpenes, measurable effects are produced in our bodies. For example, terpenes are antibacterial. Research demonstrates that they are effective in combating respiratory tract pathogens, E. coli, and in breast cancer chemoprevention. Scientists also argue that terpenes are neuroprotective: in other words, they act as chemical modulators of nervous system damage, helping protect and regenerate nerve cells.[19] Inhaling the scent of trees re-makes us at the cellular level. Just as the act of speaking facilitates human connection through linguistic abstraction (making use of our sense of hearing and mobilizing air to transmit sound waves), terpenes constitute an arboreal mode of communication through biochemical signaling (making use of our sense of smell and mobilizing air to transmit volatile organic compounds).[20] Terpenes are thus an example of a multi-sensorial mode of communication that transcends the limited perceptual range of digital visual technologies, which rely on the sense of sight.

This example illustrates an important point for scholars engaged in representing the Anthropocene: our experience of forests is multi-sensorial and embodied, but our representations of those same forests impacted by the Anthropocene are largely visual and disembodied. For example, trees affected by climate change emit different, or fewer, terpenes maladapted to new pests and predators in dynamic anthropogenically influenced processes of ecological change. Visual representations can capture only part of this complex set of processes, which are olfactory (and indeed sometimes sonified) as well as visual.

Skeptical readers may ask: by emitting terpenes, are trees engaging in self-representation? To begin to formulate an answer, consider Aldo Leopold's famous question, "how do mountains think?"[21] In exploring responses to this question, Jennifer Wenzel reminds us of the dangers of imposing anthropocentric qualities onto the nonhuman world. Through her critique of literary personification, Wenzel cautions against modes of representation that evacuate the radical alterity of nature in order to substitute it with human values, intentions, and desires.[22] This sleight of hand, she argues, is profoundly un-ecological: in seeking to acknowledge the agency of nonhumans, human modes of representation may (ironically) obscure nature's autonomy. We argue that planetary voyeurism is guilty of this fallacy. By envisioning Earth as an object that can be "seen" and understood in its entirety, planetary voyeurism occludes the possibility of nature's autonomy. In this way, it appears to empower designers and geographers to "see" the

catastrophic effect of the Anthropocene. Yet by privileging the visual apprehension of environmental degradation over more relational and multi-sensorial forms of knowledge, planetary voyeurism reduces the designer or geographer to a detached voyeur: all-knowing, all-seeing, yet sensing little or nothing.

It would be unfair of us to critique planetary voyeurism on the grounds that it over-simplifies complex socio-natural relations through visual representation. Indeed, all modes of representation require some degree of abstraction and simplification (whether in the form of digital data, vocalized language, or terpenes released into the air). Rather, we offer our analogy to draw attention to the risk of reducing nature's representational agency to questions of metaphor or aesthetics. We have also drawn a distinction between planetary voyeurism's technical visualizations versus embodied forms of multi-sensory apprehension. Our vast geospatial datasets and powerful computational tools convince us of our ability to experience and "know" the world through technologically-mediated vision. But in many instances this experience is uni-dimensional. Digital visualizations require us to simplify and abstract the vibrant materiality of the world. They deny us the biophysical presence and radical otherness of the nonhuman. In this sense, we eschew conventional forms of digital visualization not to assert the superiority of "nature experience" over representation (thereby invoking a false binary). Rather, we seek to provoke a dialogue about how we might deploy technical intermediaries to more fully engage with modalities of multi-sensorial representation and distributed agency.

Why does this matter? Our concern is that, like the Greek *pharmakon* that provides both a remedy and a poison, the production of endless visualizations of environmental catastrophe satisfies our desire to confront the Anthropocene, yet redirects creative attention away from the critical task of designing a more just and sustainable future. We critique the notion that more complex visualizations—more technology, more sensors, more data will produce a deeper understanding of environmental change. Calling for more data merely depoliticizes the Anthropocene as a primarily technical challenge. This depoliticization is, we feel, so ubiquitous as to seem entirely unremarkable; we often overlook the ironic fact that digital visual techniques developed by industrial sectors to extract resources and architect the technosphere are the same ones used by planetary voyeurs to apprehend, depict, and engage with processes of ecological degradation.[23]

Our reference to Duchamp's artwork at the outset raises several questions. Will future generations feel a similar sense of unease when they look at our visualizations of environmental degradation? Will the inherent violence, anthropocentrism, and speciesism embedded in our visualizations be as obvious in the future as the misogyny of this Duchamp artwork is to us today? Those who offer affirmative answers to these questions (as we do) might feel called upon to explore more integrative visual practices that "see" the Anthropocene in different ways. A lively debate over these issues has been underway in geography since the mid-1990s, and responses to these critiques have fundamentally altered the visual, technical, and intellectual trajectory of GIScience (leading, for example, to new techniques such as participatory GIS and counter-mapping).[24] The design disciplines would, we feel, benefit from a similar debate and parallel innovations.

This is not to say that we should abandon the possibilities offered to us through emerging visual technologies. Rather, we must remain attentive to the fact that these technologies are cultural artifacts that interpellate us toward specific beliefs, attitudes, desires, and practices. Failure to acknowledge and contextualize the artifice of Anthropocene visualizations is tantamount to a kind of myopia. We offer this critique of planetary voyeurism as a reminder that the Anthropocene manifests itself in many different ways: some large and spectacular, and others small, intimate, but nonetheless destructive. By stepping away from the technician's lens (or peephole) and into the vibrant materiality of the world, we might find that seeing through (and with) many different perspectives can transform how we view and value our earthly relationships.

13 Adams, "Geographies of Conservation II," 341.

14 Derek Gregory, "From a View to a Kill: Drones and Late Modern War," *Theory, Culture & Society* 28, no. 7-8 (2011): 190.

15 Arturo Escobar, *Designs for the Pluriverse: Radical Interdependence, Autonomy, and the Making of Worlds* (Duke University Press, 2018).

16 SCAPE Landscape Architecture, "Living Breakwaters," *Designing Our Future: Sustainable Landscapes*, https://www.asla.org/sustainablelandscapes/breakwaters.html.

17 Gregory, "From a View to a Kill," 196.

18 This is an insight long recognized in Indigenous knowledge, which Western science is recently (re)discovering. See, for example, Robin Wall Kimmerer, *Braiding Sweetgrass: Indigenous Wisdom, Scientific Knowledge and the Teachings of Plants* (Milkweed Editions, 2013); Andrea C. McCormick, et al., "Herbivore Induced Volatile Emission in Black Poplar: Regulation and Role in Attracting Herbivore Enemies," *Plant, Cell & Environment* 37, no. 8 (2014): 1909–23; Marcel Dicke & Ian T. Baldwin, "The Evolutionary Context for Herbivore-Induced Plant Volatiles: Beyond the 'Cry for Help'," *Trends in Plant Science* 15, no. 3 (2010): 167–75.

19 Sara A. Burt & Robert D. Reinders, "Antibacterial Activity of Selected Plant Essential Oils Against *Escherichia coli* O157: H7," *Letters in Applied Microbiology* 36.3 (2003): 162–67; Hyun-Joo Chang, Hyun Jung Kim & Hyang Sook Chun, "Quantitative Structure–Activity Relationship (QSAR) for Neuroprotective Activity of Terpenoids," *Life Sciences* 80, no. 9 (2007): 835–41; Thangaiyan Rabi & Anupam Bishayee, "Terpenoids and Breast Cancer Chemoprevention," *Breast Cancer Research and Treatment* 115.2 (2009): 223–39; Shigeharu Inouye, Toshio Takizawa & Hideyo Yamaguchi, "Antibacterial Activity of Essential Oils and their Major Constituents Against Respiratory Tract Pathogens by Gaseous Contact," *Journal of Antimicrobial Chemotherapy* 47, no. 5 (2001): 565–73.

20 Trees also communicate in other ways, for example through mycorrhizal networks. Marc-Andre Selosse, et. al., "Mycorrhizal Networks: Des Liaisons Dangereuses?" *Trends in Ecology & Evolution* 21, no. 11 (2006): 621–28; Suzanne Simard et al., "Net Transfer of Carbon Between Ectomycorrhizal Tree Species in the Field," *Nature* 388, no. 6642 (1997): 579.

21 Aldo Leopold, *A Sand County Almanac, and Sketches Here and There* (Oxford University Press, 1949).

22 Jennifer Wenzel, "Planet vs. Globe," *English Language Notes* 52, no. 1 (2014): 24.

23 Goldcorp, "Disrupt Mining," https://disruptmining.com/ (accessed July 22, 2019).

24 Sarah Elwood, "Critical Issues in Participatory GIS: Deconstructions, Re-constructions, and New Research Directions," *Transactions in GIS* 10, no. 5 (2006): 693–708; Jim Thatcher, et al., "Revisiting Critical GIS," *Environment and Planning A* 48, no. 5 (2016): 815–24; Nancy Peluso, "Whose Woods are These? Counter Mapping Forest Territories in Kalimantan, Indonesia," *Antipode* 27, no. 4 (1995): 383–406.

RANIA GHOSN

UNCOMMON PLANET

GEOSTORIES OF THE GLOBAL COMMONS

Rania Ghosn is associate professor of architecture and urbanism at MIT and founding partner of DESIGN EARTH with El Hadi Jazairy. Her research charts the geographies of urban systems to speculate on the techno-environment in the age of climate change. The work of DESIGN EARTH has been exhibited at the Venice Biennale and collected by MoMA. She is author of *Geographies of Trash* (2015) and *Geostories: Another Architecture for the Environment* (2018), and editor of *New Geographies 2: Landscapes of Energy* (2010).

✚ ARCHITECTURE, CLIMATOLOGY, TECHNOLOGY

"[N]o sooner had the contours of the earth emerged as a real globe—not just sensed as myth, but apprehensible as fact and measurable as space—than there arose a wholly new and hitherto unimaginable problem: the spatial ordering of the earth in terms of international law."[1]

Who governs and owns the oceans, outer space, the Earth's atmosphere, and biodiversity? The answer "everyone and no one" is the recurring paradox of the global commons today. The enclosure of the Earth into categories of territory has constructed an all-encompassing way of dividing up the planet, with the central category of sovereignty and remainder categories of *res nullius*, *res communis*, and common heritage of mankind.[2] The global commons thus first arose as a default zone in international law, conceptualized as the ungovernable outside of the international legal order of territorial states. The legacies of this geography, however, make visible the slippages between the two legal notions of territory outside sovereign states: *res nullius* and *res communis*. The former relates to territory unclaimed by a sovereign state and is therefore subject to lawful appropriation by a state with the military, political, and economic power to establish and enforce its claim – the colonial proclamation of *terra nullius* was used by European states to dispossess Indigenous peoples of their land.[3] The latter, *res communis*, refers to areas such as the deep seabed, outer space, and Antarctica, which are referred to as global commons and are not subject to the national jurisdiction of a particular state but are shared by other states, if not humanity or the international community as a whole.

In practice, however, the outside status of the global commons has often been a legal fiction. Caught in the paradox of modern enclosure, these international areas and their state of affairs might be better described as the tragedy of *res nullius* with their resources increasingly more open on a "first come, first served basis." Why has the international order of the global commons so often failed to manage things for the benefit of all humankind? "Commons," as David Harvey points out, always implies some degree of enclosure.[4] The opposite concepts of "enclosure" and "commons," as with all binaries, end up converging, with the former encroaching on and destroying the latter as extractivism intensifies and expands.[5] Once the commons "system" is dismantled, it is only a matter of time until the valuation regime that privileges the internalization of private gains—resource values, and the actors interested in claiming ownership—slowly erodes the domains that had been hitherto ruled by laws of exception. Far from leading to common good, the global commons become the subject and site of contestation in deeply unequal and unsettled sets of spatial relations, in which powerful states and transnational private actors hold the monopoly of resources, violence, and diplomacy. In a world order of extractive valuation regimes, the global commons might be most salient as a microcosm of uncommon interests.

How can we convert into image and narrative the "tragedy of the global commons" as a projective chapter in the Earth's modern history of enclosure and dispossession? The crisis of governing the global commons is that it requires both planetary re-presentation

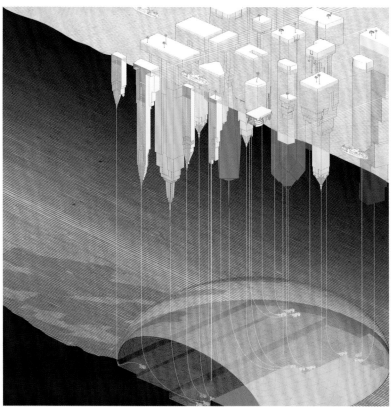

Top: Pacific Aquarium – Parliament of Refugees.
Bottom: Pacific Aquarium – Below the Water Towers.

and commoning: both a political assembly and a geographic imagination of the Earth. Such a double representational challenge brings forth tensions within the concept of the commons, as well as divergence or opposition between the globe and the Earth: "There is no planet Earth corresponding to the Promised Land of globalization," as Bruno Latour put it bluntly.[6] Globalization is the abstract space of optimized enclosure, resources, and capital flows. Similarly, the legal rhetoric that supports and legitimates dispossession of the global commons is undergirded by a spatial imaginary of abstract, vacant, empty space, with a similar narrative plot of epic conquest. If abstract space is first an act of geographical violence through which virtually every space in the world is depopulated, quantified, and exchanged on global markets, then a radical imagination counters abstraction through the primacy of geography.

In her book, *In Catastrophic Times*, Isabelle Stengers argues that industrial and extractive activities in the service of capital have provoked Gaia and produced her current "intrusion." In terms of political ecology, the planetary figure of Gaia, which shares with *geo-* the same etymology from the chthonic divinity Gè without the stalemate of disciplinary anchoring, is a conceptual tool to disquiet, to provoke, to make people think anew about globalism's ecological violence.[7] For Stengers, the current state of affairs is maintained by forms of governance that manifest as a stupefying sense of political realism, which works to evacuate politics from governance. The choice of futures has narrowed to the single infernal alternative of barbarism between runaway climate change and a geoengineered future, which both hold the planet hostage to private interests. The solution to the impasse of capitalist realism begins with the intrusion of Gaia. Away from the maintenance and protection of a ruptured international order, such "cosmopolitical proposal" asks of politics to engage those precise disagreements on how to organize the world as common – things, technologies, values, and stories.[8]

How can a planetary issue be reclaimed from expertise, whether scientific or legal, and become a "common" question, in the sense of providing the basis for political collectivity? The following *Geostories* by DESIGN EARTH are speculative fictions that dwell in the gap between climate emergency and the narrow repertoire of political responses.[9] The geostories do not say what ought to be, rather they make visible the controversies and slippages of the global commons, in what might be best described as a geographic imagination of

an uncommon planet. Thus, each of the geostories– Ocean Floor, Antarctica, Outer Space–seeks a slightly different awareness of the situation of a global common, not to lament the transgression of another enclosure of the planet, but to put in question the very same infrastructure of private gains that undergirds practices of ecocide *throughout* the planet. Beyond concerns of "political realism," commoning socializes technical issues and asks that they respond to broader interests. By contesting what "the facts" can mean, and who can interpret them, commoning refuses the depoliticization of problems by articulating a community of the problem.

To tell the three geostories of global commons is to insist on the sheer wreak and destruction of *res nullius*, which permeates geographies of *res communis*. Arguably, such geostories of global commons have special pertinence today at a moment when the common good of the planet is at stake. In the context of a breakneck climate crisis, the imperative is for the planet to overwrite the globe.[10] This would mean not only foregoing a planetary agreement on the climate but also soliciting alternative geographic imaginations. Away from the trope of the globe, the geo-politics of climate change requires aesthetic work to reclaim the Earth; a geographical imagination that is grounded, situated, material, volumetric, populated, heterogeneous, and mythical. The geographic imagination tells us that we must persistently educate ourselves into the messy negotiations and power asymmetries that surround the question of how we inhabit the Earth; a geostory renders private interests into public debate, and opens up the imagination to what is possible. It works as a "commoning agent" in the form of a disjunctive space where incommensurable geographical imaginaries speak to each other. To tell the story of global commons is thus not to reinforce measures of protection *within*, but rather to narrate a synecdoche of a global order that legitimizes environmental violence throughout.

Ocean Floor: Pacific Aquarium

The ocean seabed is the site of countries and international corporations racing to claim its rare earth mineral resources for the production of batteries and alloys. As early as 1873, the expedition of HMS Challenger discovered that the deep seabed contains valuable mineral resources, in particular the polymetallic or manganese nodules. The 1956 First United Nations Convention of the Law of the Sea had reaffirmed that the high seas and seabed were a geography of non-possession, with free access for all. In 1967, Arvid Pardo, the Maltese ambassador to the

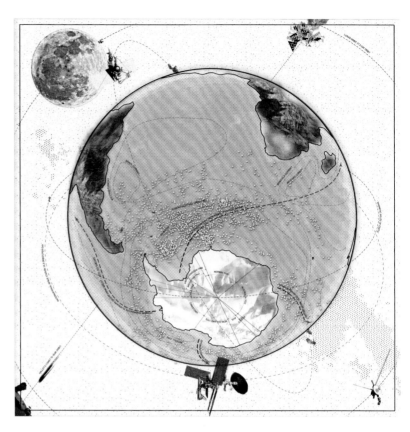

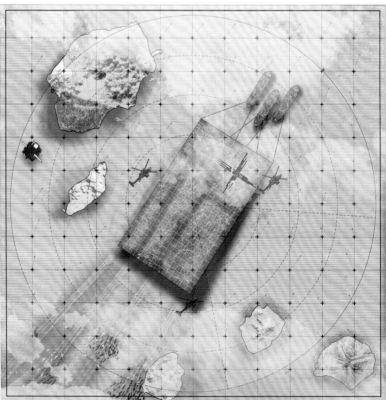

Top: Of Oil And Ice – At the Bottom of the World.
Bottom: Of Oil And Ice – Iceberg Calving.

United Nations, argued that the *res communis* of the seabed would entail the tragedy of the commons. In order to prevent the "first come, first served" regime that would have favored advanced industrialized countries, the Global South, under the auspices of the United Nations, advocated the establishment of an international regime in which any resource extraction would have to benefit the international community as a whole. The seabed that remains outside of national jurisdictions, called the "Area" in the United Nations Convention on the Law of the Sea, is legally part of the "common heritage of mankind," which, following UN General Assembly Resolution 2749, should not be subject to national appropriation. The Area is under the legal mandate of the International Seabed Authority (ISA), which was created in 1982 with the mission to oversee exploration, mapping, and resource management in the high seas. Since 2001, however, ISA has granted 12 exploration licenses for minerals on the Clarion-Clipperton Zone deep seabed, an area in the Pacific Ocean approximately the size of Europe with the world's largest deposits of deep-seabed rare earth minerals.

The project "Pacific Aquarium" makes visible the externalities of the seabed extraction—plumes, species extinction and proliferation—as well as the promises and limits of currently envisioned geoengineering solutions.[11] At the ocean floor the sharply toothed, comb-like suction machines churn and rip the ocean surface into sediment slurry, which if not contained would distribute widely through deep ocean currents. In "Below the Water Towers," a catchment dome caps mining activities to contain sediment plumes. Polluted water is separated from surrounding water and transported into a series of inverted water towers just below the surface for processing. Purified water is gradually released back into the ocean. "Hanging Gardens of the Pacific" responds to ISA mandates concerning the conservation of the flora and fauna in the CCZ mining area. Suspended by cables from a grid of surficial floats, a terraforming infrastructure relocates linear transects of substrate samples to incubate a benthic ecosystem that will be grafted onto the depleted seabed once mining is completed.

Antarctica: Of Oil and Ice

Before the 1957 International Geophysical Year, Antarctica, and based on acts of imperial exploration, five nations—Australia, France, Britain, New Zealand, and Norway—had laid claims to portions of the Earth's only continent without a native human population. The 1959 Antarctic Treaty System "froze" national claims to sectors on the southern continent and regulated international relations with respect to Antarctica. The treaty, entering into effect in 1961

and currently having 50 signatory nations, sets aside Antarctica as a scientific preserve, establishes freedom of scientific investigation and bans military activity on that continent. This includes regimes for the management of fishing resources in the Southern Ocean, as well as a comprehensive environmental protection protocol signed at Madrid in 1991.

The project "Of Oil and Ice" weaves together two concerns brought forth by climate change—melting glaciers in Antarctica and energy intensive desalination industries in the Arabian Gulf—in a proposal to haul icebergs from Antarctica to Hormuz Strait.[12] Antarctica annually calves approximately 93% of the world's total iceberg mass—an estimated 326 quadrillion gallons of freshwater. Icebergs are *res nullius* – legally free for the taking without interference from national or international regulatory bodies. A large tabular iceberg, which best resists rolling or tipping, is captured and towed to the Arabian Peninsula at a cost considerably less than that of fresh water from desalination plants. The speculative proposal foregrounds how the future of Antarctica hinges on planetary contracts, such as the 2015 Paris Agreement on climate change. If such treaties are not put into effect, the melting of Antarctica promises to be a spectacular vanishing act, with the world's ears tuned in to a cold seltzer sound – high-pitched hissing, squealing, popping, and creaking with stress under the pressures of international competition over resources.

Outer Space: Cosmorama

In the early 1950s the legal geography of the Earth remained as it had been since the 1648 Peace of Westphalia: the Earth's land—and the airspace above that land—was the legal possession of states. The Cold War prompted the 1967 Outer Space Treaty, which declared that outer space, including the Moon and other celestial bodies, "shall be the province of mankind" and stipulated that these areas are "not subject to national appropriation by claim of sovereignty, by means of use or occupation, or by any other means."[13]

Space has gained renewed significance with nascent private space commodity initiatives speculating in off-sourced extractive industries for water, platinum group metals, and other resource riches. Commercial actors of this "New Space Age," such as SpaceX and Planetary Resources, are set to mine valuable resources from near-Earth asteroids and bring "the natural resources of space within humanity's economic sphere."[14] Asteroids could be the new equities! Aside from the daunting logistics, the

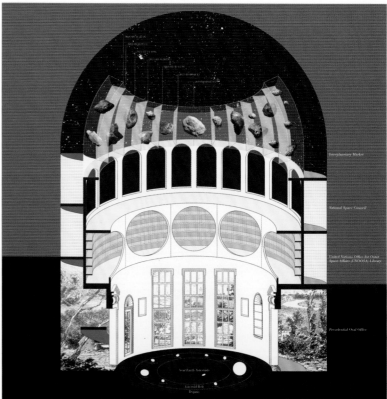

Top: Cosmorama – Cosmic Rushmore.
Bottom: Cosmorama – Architecture of the New Space Age.

largest Earthbound obstacle to space mining is the 1967 Outer Space Treaty (OST). In a desire to facilitate the expansion of private extractive industries into extra-planetary space, the recent 2015 US SPACE Act, or the Spurring Private Aerospace Competitiveness and Entrepreneurship Act, recognized the right of US citizens to engage in the commercial exploitation of resources in outer space, "First in time, first in right" is again applied to Outer Space.

From Cosmorama (2018), the triptych "Mining the Sky" describes and speculates on the franchisement of asteroid extraction to private corporations. Drawing together the Architecture of the New Space Age, the conceptual section makes visible the intertwined and conflicting interests of the United States, the United Nations, and space industry and investors. Robotic arms are used to process the asteroid: they either hollow out the asteroid, collecting the trail of debris in the fabricated cave or mine the surface to carve out the face of the gods of the New Space Age into a cosmic Mount Rushmore constellation.

1 Carl Schmitt, *The Nomos of the Earth in the International Law of the Jus Publicum Europaeum* (Telos Press, 2003 [1950]), 86.

2 First introduced in the late 1960s as an alternative understanding of jurisdiction that would prevent both appropriation and unbridled exploitation, World Heritage of Mankind requires that the resources of a territory be held and utilized on behalf of the international community as a whole, with special attention to the needs of its most vulnerable members.

3 *Res nullius* (in Roman law) were either things unappropriated by anyone, such as things in common, unoccupied lands, wild animals; or things which cannot be appropriated: sacred things dedicated to the celestial gods; religious things dedicated to underworld gods; and sanctified things, such as the walls and gates of a city.

4 David Harvey, "The Future of the Commons," *Radical History Review* 109 (2011): 101–07.

5 Mario Blaser & Marisol de la Cadena, "The Uncommons: An Introduction," *Anthropologica* 59 (2017): 185–93.

6 Bruno Latour, "Terroir, Globe, Earth – A New Political Triangle," http://www.bruno-latour.fr/sites/default/files/downloads/2016-01-3-TERRITORIES-GB.pdf.

7 Bruno Latour, "Why Gaia is not a God of Totality," *Theory, Culture & Society* 34, no. 2-3 (2016): 61–81.

8 Isabelle Stengers, *In Catastrophic Times: Resisting the Coming Barbarism* (Open Humanities Press, 2015), 54.

9 Ibid. Also, Isabelle Stengers, "The Cosmopolitical Proposal," in B. Latour & P. Weibel (eds) *Making Things Public* (MIT Press, 2005), 994–1003; Rania Ghosn & El Hadi Jazairy, *Geostories: Another Architecture for the Environment* (Actar, 2018).

10 Gayatri Chakravorty Spivak, "Imperative to Reimagine the Planet," *An Aesthetic Education in the Era of Globalization* (Harvard University Press, 2012), 335–50.

11 Rania Ghosn & El Hadi Jazairy, "Leviathan in the Aquarium," *Journal of Architectural Education* 71, no. 2 (2017): 271–79.

12 Rania Ghosn & El Hadi Jazairy, "Of Oil and Ice," *Science Fiction Studies* 45, no. 3 (2018): 433–39.

13 See Fraser MacDonald, "Anti-Astropolitik Outer Space and the Orbit of Geography," *Progress in Human Geography* 31, no. 5 (2007): 592–615. Note: In the same month that OST became open for signature (January 1967), NASA officials visited Antarctica in order to learn about maintaining human exploration in a harsh environment, on one of the two remaining "last frontiers." Because of its environment, Antarctica was considered an "ideal testing ground" for equipment, infrastructure, and logistics that might be used in outer space.

14 Amir Efrati, "Start-Up Outlines Asteroid-Mining Strategy," *The Wall Street Journal* (April 24, 2012), https://www.wsj.com/articles/SB100 01424052702303459004577364110378178038.

UNCONVENTIONAL RESOURCES

MATTHEW RANSOM

Matthew Ransom is a designer and researcher based in New York City. His work focuses on uncovering the many ways in which architecture manifests itself, and in the politics of representation. This interest has led to work with organizations such as Alphabet's Sidewalk Labs, the Columbia University GSAPP Incubator at the New Museum, and the Storefront for Art and Architecture. Matthew is currently the design director of Overhead, an architectural design studio founded in 2018.

+ GEOLOGY, TECHNOLOGY, GEOSCIENCES

Previous: Drilling tower and flare illuminated at night, Susquehanna County, PA.

Above: Fracking pad spotted through the trees, Susquehanna County, PA.

It's an image so familiar that it's more archetypical than cliché: a weathervane, perched somewhere atop a rural outbuilding, gently swaying to the unseen forces of the breeze. It might not look like much—and it might look like a rooster—but it engenders an expanded sensitivity, another dimension to the environment that before the advent of numerical climate modeling would have otherwise remained unknowable.

Far less familiar but, today, no less rural: a polychromatic array of 4-D analytics, interpreting environmental conditions miles above and below ground, swaying in the breeze at 57,000 bits per second. Since 2005, northeastern Pennsylvania has been infiltrated by dozens of oil and gas companies vying for access to the vast Marcellus shale deposits running deep underground.[1] Its attendant technologies for both prospecting and extraction have fundamentally transformed the rural fabric into something truly strange. As the industry and its environmental impact take hold, the landscape is being transformed in dimensions that are often difficult to perceive, and difficult to inhabit, without the right tools. And like the weathervane, residents of the region have begun to develop new ways to attune themselves, new sensitivities to these emergent landscapes.

Breaking Ground

After a century of frenzied fossil fuel consumption, oil seeps and fountains of "black gold" are only the stuff of movies.[2] The industry increasingly looks to "unconventional resources" to meet global energy demands and, unsurprisingly, these resources require unconventional means and methods.[3] Hydraulic fracturing, or "fracking" as it is conventionally known, is a technique used in natural gas extraction whereby pressurized (and proprietary) fluids and millions of gallons of water are injected into boreholes, fracturing the rock and releasing pockets of gas trapped deep below ground.[4] These fractures are filled with proppant, or "frac sand," to facilitate the flow of gas into the well.

The technique is about as sophisticated as the name implies, and a simple online search yields video demonstrations of "frac guns": perforated metal canisters attached to long hoses, hissing and spewing as befits something from deep below ground. In fact, hydraulic fracturing is nothing new. It has been used for years as a means of stimulating conventional deposits – petroleum reservoirs trapped beneath a layer of impermeable rock. What has brought fracking above ground and into the public imaginary is that when paired with coeval advances in directional drilling technology and remote sensing, it becomes the key to unlocking previously inaccessible, and incalculable, deposits of hydrocarbons trapped in pockets of rich, porous shale. These deposits are typically deemed "unconventional" because their prospective yield is difficult to determine, and their extraction entails a vast technological regime.

Whereas conventional deposits of oil and natural gas are consolidated in reservoirs that lie within relatively easy reach, shale gas is trapped miles below ground, across broad swaths of land: drilling a simple vertical well would yield negligible results. Unsurprisingly, developing new wells capable of extracting such deposits is an expensive endeavor – the average cost of well development in the Marcellus Shale today is in excess of five million dollars.[5] These costs, coupled with the difficulty of projecting returns, make fracking a high-risk endeavor. And so in an effort to mitigate risk, oil and gas companies have developed an extraordinary arsenal of tools to locate, index, and extract shale gas. These tools span from the upper reaches of our atmosphere, to the depths of the Earth's crust, engaging geophysics, chemical engineering, remote sensing, data science, and a host of other fields.[6]

Homing In

Long before the trees are cleared and the equipment arrives, the site of a new well has likely been analyzed from hundreds of miles above ground by satellites like the USGS

1 See Pennsylvania's Governor's *Marcellus Shale Advisory Commission 2011 Report*, (July 2011), http://files.dep.state.pa.us/PublicParticipation/MarcellusShaleAdvisoryCommission/MarcellusShaleAdvisoryPortalFiles/MSAC_Final_Report.pdf.

2 Most notably, writer and director Paul Thomas Anderson's 2007 film, *There Will Be Blood*.

3 For an outline of unconventional resources as relates to fracking, see ExxonMobil's shareholder report from 2014, "Unconventional Resources Development – Managing the Risks," (September 2014), https://cdn.exxonmobil.com/~/media/global/files/energy-and-environment/unconventional_resources_development_risk_management_report.pdf.

4 USGS.gov, "How Much Water Does the Typical Hydraulically Fractured Well Require?" https://www.usgs.gov/faqs/how-much-water-does-typical-hydraulically-fractured-well-require?qt-news_science_products=0#qt-news_science_products (accessed August 5, 2019).

5 Based on estimates from The U.S. Energy Information Administration's "Trends in U.S. Oil and Natural Gas Upstream Costs," EIA Independent Statistics & Analysis (March 2016), https://www.eia.gov/analysis/studies/drilling/pdf/upstream.pdf.

6 For an outline of how these interact, see *Managing Drilling Risk*, in the Oil Field Review, accessed on Schlumberger's site: https://www.slb.com/-/media/files/oilfield-review/manage (accessed August 5, 2019).

7 For an outline of specifications, including some dazzling imagery, see the United States Geological Survey's site: http://landsat.usgs.gov/landsat8.php (accessed August 5, 2019).

Landsat 8, which offer high-resolution, multispectral images that reveal mineral and vegetal surface conditions.[7] For a certain price, private mapping and exploration companies can request that the gaze of these satellites periodically be directed to a particular sweep of land, enabling temporal analysis of minute (within a millimeter) deformations of the Earth's surface. These deformations signal geologic activity, and can also be used to track oil spills.[8] Weirdly, the same lens that is used to locate potential new sites of hydrocarbon exploration is often the same lens that reveals the extent of environmental impact when such exploration is successful.[9]

Homing in on particular areas for well development, industry geologists rely upon a combination of aeromagnetic and lidar surveys to assess potential sites for further analysis.[10] From a vantage point as high as 3,000 feet, lidar scanners and magnetometers affixed to small planes, helicopters, or drones produce three-dimensional data accurate up to one foot.[11] These images can have an uncanny quality to them. Because lidar scans penetrate tree canopies, they can produce images—constructed from point clouds—that are shorn of all vegetation, laying bare the Earth's surface, revealing hidden faults. And through a similar irony as the remote sensing mentioned above, this technology is not only an essential tool for the petroleum industry but it has also become instrumental in forest management. Should one decide to view the Earth beyond its mineral potential, lidar imaging offers a view of both the forest and all its trees – forest health is tracked by assessing the height and diameter of individual trees.[12]

To supplement this data, aeromagnetic surveys trace invisible fluctuations in the Earth's magnetic field, which indicate the nature of mineral deposits and provide a basis for estimating their depth. Flying in a grid, the surveying aircraft traces a path that determines the resolution of the map, and the degree to which the information between its flights' paths will need to be interpolated into a continuous whole.[13] And yet, after all this reconnaissance—after detailed maps have been drawn and the landscape has been subsumed into this instrumental logic—there comes a time when industry geologists must make contact with the surface, and necessarily, with landowners.

In order to confirm what from above can only be intuited, industry geologists rely upon a variety of on-the-ground (or below it) technologies that require real access to the land. It is often with a knock on the door that they announce themselves. The force behind this knock is tens of thousands of dollars worth of initial surveys and data collection and, at stake, many millions more. Once an access agreement is reached, a grid will again be overlaid across the landscape as a matrix of geophones installed to detect signals from vibroseis trucks, called "thumpers."[14] The space between each sensor represents an area of uncertainty and a projection that will later be collated into a comprehensive form; denser grids provide higher-resolution data, but at greater time and cost. The process is so time consuming and expensive, sometimes costing hundreds of thousands of dollars, that these surveys are closely guarded within the industry. But the information they provide is essential. Seismic reflection surveys can reach as deep as 10,000 feet below grade, and they provide both two- and three-dimensional data that will be translated into a graphical interface, providing the basis for statistical modeling and strategic planning.[15] As the vibrations are swept up into a network of sensors, a subterranean landscape comes into view – and it does so with images that could easily be mistaken for MRIs. From here, drilling rigs will be mobilized to make first contact with this subterranean landscape and, from the moment they breach the surface, a remarkable exchange between inference and evidence occurs.

Geosteering

If modern drill heads are a contemporary analogue to a coal miner's pickax, they are also the miner's eyes and ears: both behind the drill head and within pipe fittings, elaborate instrumentation monitors a variety of subsurface conditions such as magnetic resonance, resistivity, and neutron porosity.[16] As the drill grinds its way through miles of the Earth's crust, technicians above ground can watch progress in real time. And through a process known as "geosteering," the direction of the drilling can be manipulated, giving drill operators the capacity to explore the subterranean landscape from miles above.[17]

In northeastern Pennsylvania, these sites are tucked behind the trees so that, at least from the road, they all but disappear from view. Yet, for as sophisticated as it might sound, there is nothing rarified about a drill pad: endless fleets of diesel trucks spew exhaust as their engines rev and the well is pressurized; open pits of discharge from the well reflect a murky sky; and deep underground, a pneumatic gun relentlessly breaks apart layers of the Earth's crust, releasing gases from the final resting place of organisms many millions years old.

Miles down the road in anonymous office buildings, feedback from the well, along with many others, is collated at regional command centers. It is from this vantage point that a new landscape begins to emerge. Here, behind mirrored glass and dropped ceilings, energy companies like Cabot and Halliburton use advanced analytics to gather millions of data points from various sources: from high above ground and deep below it; from past returns and explorations, to present conditions and projected ones; from geospatial information to historical maps. All of this is drawn together using proprietary software like Dynamic Graphics Inc.'s CoViz 4D, or Halliburton's DecisionSpace 365, which provide four-dimensional interfaces for strategic planning and drilling operations. With these tools, engineers can navigate landscapes of past and present conditions, combined with projected risks and returns; wild arrays of color overlay seismic reflectance models, with pie charts hovering beside hydra-like tangles of drill paths.[18] They provide a Latourian flat plane to gather seemingly disparate information together so that new associations can be revealed – feedback from one developed well can inform the drill path of the next.[19] Because

these interfaces interpolate between observed conditions (i.e., historical well data and on-site monitoring) and projected ones (statistical models driven by these observations), they are difficult to categorize. They are one part facsimile, and another part living landscape, accessible only through the combined data streams of countless sources. They are also remarkably similar to what climatologists use to predict weather patterns.[20] With their staggering complexity and their arsenal of high-resolution sensors, it would be easy to miss that these spaces are devoid of one critical agent – somewhere, thousands of feet above the shale, residents in areas of fracking struggle to mount evidence that the fabric of their lives has fundamentally changed.

Reports of tap water running black, or of methane in the water being set aflame, are common, as are reports of sick children and dying livestock.[21] Despite having a connection to the land that often spans generations, people like Stacey Haney in Eliza Griswold's deeply reported *Amity and Prosperity*, find themselves at the center of conversations about what constitutes truth or evidence of what's happening there. Against the 4-D analytics of a control room, low-fi accounts of methane levels in a household's drinking water, such as were encountered on my visit to Susquehanna County (with Andres Jaque's studio at Columbia University during the fracking boom in 2016) fail to hold much weight.

One of the residents we met had grown so accustomed to fluctuations of methane in his water that he had outfitted his basement with an elaborate system that allowed him to modulate between various drinking wells and a freshwater reserve in his basement – a plastic bladder, fit between some plastic lawn chairs and bric-a-brac, that is manually refilled via a tube that winds out of the basement through a small hole in the door and into the yard. The levels of methane were as unpredictable as the activity on the drill pad just up the hill from his house (from where he had been receiving some royalties). He kept track of both the royalties and the methane

8 Rebecca Lasica, "A New Age for Oil and Gas Exploration: Remote-Sensing Data and Analytics Are Changing the Industry," *Earth Imaging Journal* (July 4, 2015), http://eijournal.com/print/articles/a-new-age-for-oil-and-gas-exploration-remote-sensing-data-and-analytics-are-changing-the-industry.

9 See the USGS and NASA's online guide, "Landsat Climate Change Fact Sheet," https://landsat.gsfc.nasa.gov/wp-content/uploads/2013/02/LandsatClimateChangeFactSheet.pdf (accessed August 5, 2019).

10 Lidar, or Light Detection and Ranging, is a surveying method that uses light in the form of a pulsed laser to measure variable distances to the Earth.

11 Hans-Erik Andersen & Demetrios Gatziolis, "A Guide to LIDAR Data Acquisition and Processing for the Forests of the Pacific Northwest," *United States Department of Agriculture* (July 2008), https://www.fs.fed.us/pnw/pubs/pnw_gtr768.pdf.

12 Maggi Kelly & Stefania Di Tommaso, "Mapping Forests with Lidar Provides Flexible, Accurate Data with Many Uses," *California Agriculture* 69, no. 1 (2015): 14–20.

13 For an exhaustive guide to hydrocarbon exploration, see Norman J. Hyne, *Nontechnical Guide to Petroleum Geology, Exploration, Drilling, and Production* (Penn Well, 2001).

14 Ibid.

15 Ibid.

16 Halliburton, "Logging-While-Drilling (LWD)," https://www.halliburton.com/en-US/ps/sperry/drilling/lwd.html?node-id=hfyjrqtw (accessed August 5, 2019).

levels in his family's water using what appeared to be an outdated version of Microsoft Excel. And though the numbers danced around, it would be difficult to draw correlations between gas activity up the hill and methane levels down below. Nevertheless, he had grown sensitive to aspects of the environment that he had never before considered. And with or without airtight evidence, he would continue working the levers of his ad-hoc plumbing system and logging his observations from his version of a control room, lined with family photos, diplomas, and ribbons that were testament to a home well run.

This begs the question: how would the house run if it were attuned to the same spectral landscapes the oil and gas industry inhabit? What would it mean if local wisdom, and local building culture, were supplemented with data from four-dimensional decision spaces?

In a small step in that direction, grassroots organizations have begun looking to environmental monitoring technology to change the equation between technocratic oil companies and residents like this, and to bring issues of environmental impact to bear through more empirical means. Organizations like Citizen Sense, which empowers nonprofessionals with training in small-scale environmental monitoring, and SkyTruth, which uses satellite imagery to monitor environmental threats from above, are exciting developments that expand environmental sensitivity.[22] However, when compared to the landscapes of fracking, they remain limited in their resolution.

Seeing Double

Since our visit in 2016, gas prices have fallen dramatically and so the industry has had to become more efficient.[23] One of the ways it's doing that is by developing finer lenses for handling its data, and by making use of an analytical tool also used in climate modeling called a "digital twin." Hailed as the next wave of gas industry technology, digital twin software advances existing 4-D analytics by incorporating even more data, made legible with the aid of machine learning.[24] By outfitting all

17 Ulterra, "What Is Geosteering?" https://ulterra.com/oil-and-gas/what-is-geosteering [accessed August 05, 2019].

18 See Dynamic Graphics, Inc.'s promotional images from their "CoViz 4D" Software, https://www.dgi.com/coviz/cvmain.html [accessed August 5, 2019].

19 Regarding the power that comes from gathering together, through codified methods of transcription, disparate sources of information, see Bruno Latour, "Drawing Things Together," in Michael Lynch & Steve Woolgar (eds) *Representation in Scientific Practice* (MIT Press, 1990).

20 Paul Edward's history of climate modeling laid the groundwork for this piece and continues to provide a framework for understanding digital twins, remote sensing, and more: Paul N. Edwards, *A Vast Machine: Computer Models, Climate Data, and the Politics of Global Warming* (MIT Press, 2010).

21 See Eliza Griswold's Pulitzer-Prize winning, years-long reporting on the effect of the shale boom on a small Pennsylvania town: Eliza Griswold, *Amity and Prosperity: One Family and the Fracturing of America* (Farrar, Strauss and Giroux, 2018).

22 See https://citizensense.net/ and https://skytruth.org/.

23 Justin Mikulka, "Fracking 2.0 Was a Financial Disaster, Will Fracking 3.0 Be Different?" *DESMOG* (March 12, 2019), https://www.desmogblog.com/2019/03/12/shale-oil-drilling-financial-disaster-fracking-3-0.

24 Jyoti Prakash, "Digital Twins Define Oil and Gas 4.0 in the Future," ARC Advisory Group (August 7, 2018), https://www.arcweb.com/blog/digital-twins-define-oil-gas-40.

the attendant infrastructure of fracking with "Internet of Things" (IoT) sensors, digital models can become ever more closely attuned to their physical counterparts.[25] And because the number of existing wells has bloomed to hundreds of thousands, there is a mountain of data to color these digital twins.

In one promotional video, a technician orbits around the digital twin of a gas refinery. The model is built in exquisite detail, and it is updated in real time based on feedback from its IoT devices. Strangely, the model is rendered so that directional shadows play across its components.[26] And in the distance, albeit in lower resolution, rolling green hills gesture toward some specific place, but too generically rendered to feel like anywhere in particular. Driving through Susquehanna County—the locus of over a thousand active wells—one could be forgiven for thinking it a rural idyll.[27] But pause for a moment, and one might glimpse something just through the trees: a methane flare waving in the breeze; a wishing well set askew beside a turbine vent spinning wildly; elaborate instrumentation buried in the bric-a-brac of a domestic basement. For it is in places like this that some of the most critical issues of our time collide: issues of big data and inequality, of facticity and the limits of reason, and of contending with irreparable landscapes. Far from being rural, these places are the avant-garde of a future that awaits us all.

25 Suryansh Purwar, et al. "Digital Twin Implementation for Integrated Production & Reservoir Management," Halliburton white paper, https://www.ienergy.community/ Portals/1/IenergyDocs/Marketing/ DigitalTwin_Integrated_Reservoir_ Production.pdf (accessed August 5, 2019).

26 Video demonstration on Aveva's website, "Aveva Engage," https://sw.aveva.com/ engineer-procure-construct/engineering-and-design/engage (accessed August 5, 2019).

27 Marcellus Gas, "Susquehanna County," https://www.marcellusgas.org/index. php?mapsize=smaller&county_id=2&muni_ id=&company_id=&searchtext=&date_ added=&sp=1&sd=1&pw=1&sw=1&formation= (accessed August 05, 2019).

Previous: Multispectral imagery, New Milford, Susquehanna County, Pennsylvania.

Opposite (from left): Basement water reservoir; wishing well on a resident's property adjacent to a fracking well.

IN CONVERSATION WITH
JENNIFER GABRYS

Jennifer Gabrys is Chair in Media, Culture and Environment in the department of Sociology at University of Cambridge. Her research and projects investigate the intersection of environments and communication technologies. Her most recent book, *Program Earth: Environmental Sensing Technology and the Making of a Computational Planet* (2016), reveals how the use of environmental sensing technologies are "rewiring" both the individuals and the environments they monitor. **Karen M'Closkey + Keith VanDerSys** spoke with Gabrys about her recent citizen sensing projects and the role of technology in defining new environments.

+ You are trained as a landscape architect. How has that directly informed your approach to media studies?

I've had a long-standing interest in waste and waste landscapes, and have always thought about media as part of how landscapes are encountered so in that way I feel like I've continued doing landscape architecture in different formats. When I was practicing as a landscape architect in Los Angeles at Rios Associates, I worked on the Fresh Kills Landfill competition. At the same time, I was volunteering at the Center for Land Use Interpretation and we would go on bus tours around Los Angeles, into the Mojave Desert, and into Utah. It became very apparent to me that infrastructure, communication infrastructure in particular, was shaping the land and land use in particular ways. I was quite interested to see how digital technologies were making new landscapes. It was through a combined interest in digital technologies and waste that I developed the idea of a natural history of electronics to look at various parts of the electronics supply chain. The life cycle of electronics is creating new fossils and new environments, which gets to your GEO theme. I find it exciting to see how landscape architecture and media studies, as well as science and technology studies, continue to inform each other in all sorts of ways.

+ After *Digital Rubbish: A Natural History of Electronics*, you published *Accumulation: The Material Politics of Plastic*. Your more recent book, *Program Earth: Environmental Sensing Technology and the Making of a Computational Planet*, focuses less on the materials of the technologies themselves and more on the environments and relations that emerge through the use of such instruments. What led to that direction in the work?

From the inception, I've been interested in environmental technologies such as sensors along with the environmental impacts of digital media, more broadly. My thesis topic became the book *Digital Rubbish*, and some further collaborative work on plastics came out of that, which became *Accumulation*. When I moved to Goldsmiths, University of London and set up an MA in Design and Environment, I began developing my own sensor work while teaching about creative environmental sensing projects and developing pilot projects. As an outgrowth of that work, I received funding from the European Research Council [ERC] for the Citizen Sense project, which began in January 2013. Low-cost and DIY sensors were in their early stages, so they were interesting to look at from a social and critical perspective. The Citizen Sense project undertook practice-based research with communities to see how they would put these sensors to work, as well as what sort of data they would generate, and whether they would be able to effect change by taking their data to regulators. We now have ERC funding for a proof-of-concept project, Airkit, which is a toolkit for undertaking citizen-led air quality monitoring. *Program Earth* has developed as a theoretical and empirical inquiry into sensors along with this practice-based work into sensors.

+ You detail some of the nuts and bolts of how people can build and use their own sensors in your book *How to Do Things with Sensors*. What about the analysis and interpretation of the data collected through these instruments and collaborations?

Data can be one of the trickiest parts of citizen sensing: it's easy enough to roll out gadgets and have people look at instantaneous readings, but often the most meaningful aspects of sensor data can come from analyzing more extensive data sets and in relation to other environmental data.

We built a DIY data-analysis toolkit, Airsift, which allowed people to look at their sensory data along with weather data and regulatory air-quality data. With this tool, and working with participants, we developed data stories to communicate findings. We had some interesting findings; for example, rather than looking at pollution data on an annual average as the local councils tend to do, we looked at the data within a 24-hour cycle in order to see with more detail where local sources of pollution were coming from. This also allowed us to understand the possibility of acting on pollution in a much different way. We could begin to see where traffic, construction, or industry was creating particular pollution patterns, so that we might prevent or mitigate those pollution sources.

As part of the Citizen Sense project, we coedited a special issue on environmental data, and contributed a piece called, "Just Good Enough Data," coauthored with an atmospheric scientist with whom we developed a set of analytic techniques for looking at citizen data. We detailed the ways in which regulators will dismiss citizen data, and argue instead that it is "good enough" to establish patterns that can be acted and followed up on. Citizen data isn't just bringing different kinds of data sets that might be complementary to extant data – it's actually bringing different kinds of ontologies for thinking about how to gather and act on data.

+ Is citizen sensing one piece under the broader notion that you call "environmental citizenship"? That is, individuals gathering information is an important element to sensing, but looking at larger data sets is another. Are you getting the latter kind of information elsewhere compared to what individual citizens are collecting?

One of the key research questions for this project is to think about how the term "the citizen" is used quite freely and prolifically within the space of digital technology. These technologies generally promise to make better citizens of people, but these citizens are often imagined within quite streamlined and efficient processes. I want to query and critique that – to look at whether these devices fulfill their promised intentions. If not, why not? Does citizenship emerge through simply gathering information, showing it to regulators, and achieving action? I was somewhat skeptical of this diagram of political engagement, knowing just how difficult it can be to work within regulatory systems to improve environments. So, this is what the project was trying to find out by investigating sensors and environmental engagement with communities. I think overall this gets to the question of how new kinds of evidentiary techniques are becoming quite central to expressions of citizenship. Digital technologies are playing a formative role in this, which allows us to potentially question how citizenship is being constructed through digital practices: what the advantages of that might be, and what the limitations of that might be, and who's able to participate in these practices and be heard.

+ Have you encountered skepticism about the validity of citizen-led data? If so, from whom?

We inevitably encountered skepticism about citizen data from regulators and people working in government, across local, state, and federal levels. It was interesting to see how, at these different levels, people would be more or less willing to think through the possibilities of sensors. The US EPA has done quite a lot of work to actually enable and facilitate citizens using sensors. They have set up an air-sensor toolbox, and they have a whole series of webinars that they run regularly to help people with environmental justice concerns to learn about processes of data integrity when working with sensors. It can often be at the local level that you encounter more skepticism about citizen data. But this can also be because regulators just don't have the resources, logistically or practically, to deal with environmental data coming from citizens.

+ You've written that sensing tools are not just descriptive of environments but are generative of them. And you argue for exploration and experimentation with instruments especially in terms of their potential to create "capacities for feeling the real." Can you say something more about that phrase?

My work is informed by pragmatist philosophy, so I'm interested in how technologies have certain kinds of world-building capacities and how they form particular material and environmental relations. Different technologies tune into environments in particular ways, and so that's where I see that they have generative and constructive qualities. They allow us to see particular temporalities of data, and make certain kinds of numerical readings of environments. What does it mean when sensors are posting data every 30 seconds, trying to create a set of readings about pollution levels in order to inform people about the reality of pollution as a problem? How does that differ from people drawing on bodily experiences of pollution, where they might take note of their asthma episodes or other health effects that cause different responses and ways of understanding the experience of pollution?

It's important to attend to all of these ways of thinking about experiences of pollution. People often turn to these kinds of devices because they feel that their own experiences don't register for regulators, so they need to create other kinds of evidence–other kinds of data–in order to be legible within a space of governance. It is interesting to see how these technologies then come into that space, allow people to create particular kinds of evidence, but then don't necessarily perform in the ways that expert-led instruments might. Their observations are entangled with their campaigns for housing developments, preserving green space, and creating more sustainable transport, so they're also using these devices to tune in to particular problems and support particular claims that they have. That's why I think there's a certain kind of "feeling for the real" here that emerges, that allows people to attend to environmental problems in ways that also might allow them to act on them.

+ We've talked about how you use sensors and work with communities to gather data. Are the ways that you visualize and spatialize the data facilitated by you having been trained as a designer?

This question of the spatialization of data is an interesting one. For our Citizen Sense project, we used maps, did fieldwork, created photo documentations, and introduced spatial questions through logbooks that asked people to think about where pollution was occurring. So, it was a kind of spatial analysis, but it was occurring in a somewhat ad hoc fashion. We were figuring out how to work with these devices, understand their effectivity, put together toolkits for people to use, understand what people's pollution concerns were, and learn atmospheric science practices all on the fly. We also, in the end, built our own custom devices since the off-the-shelf products were buggy or didn't allow us to access data for further analysis. We are further refining this infrastructure as a social technology through the Airkit project. But I think there's also another iteration of thinking about how to visualize and spatialize the data.

I know this also gets to the question about the different kinds of media and methods that landscape architects use. We're not quite doing drawings, but we are working with a broad range of sensors and other kinds of devices and platforms, producing data stories with visualizations and maps, using logbooks and making films. Here's where I think many of these methods in media are drawing on some of my design training. Much of the participatory research that I've engaged with draws on my experience of doing public engagement in landscape architecture and urban design, as well as policy and planning.

+ You have used the phrase "becoming environmental of computation." How is that different from the more commonly used "computational environment"?

Within the larger and longer context of ubiquitous computing, I was interested in thinking about how computation is moving from what Mark Weiser has described as the box-like form of the desktop computer, to become distributed in environments. For at least 30 years, computation has become more pervasive through developments such as smart environments, smart cities, smart infrastructure, smart oceans, and smart forests. So, it's important to think about how computation is changing as it becomes more environmental, infrastructural, networked, and automated. Then, on the other side, it is important to consider how environments are also shape-shifting as they become digitalized and digitized "smart" spaces.

This isn't just about different kinds of infrastructural arrangements, but about different kinds of spatial arrangements, subjects, and forms of governance that emerge. I'm particularly interested in this question of governance, and that's part of what I'm bringing into the smart forest investigation because we're finding that, for instance, forests are being articulated as natural climate solutions, and are performing as technologies of sorts. So, even environments are being turned into optimized responsive organisms, as it were, that are operating as technologies might. There's a kind of co-constitution of environments and computation that I'm trying to capture with the phrase, "becoming environmental of computation." Environment isn't the ground that computers are simply rolled out on, but that they're becoming together and creating new kinds of arrangements and relations and politics.

+ What is the smart forest project?

It's a new five-year project, also funded by the ERC, and we'll be starting our research in May [2020]. It's global in scope, and in the first instance, we'll be doing a scan of where smart forest initiatives are taking place, from New York City to Indonesia. We'll be selecting sites, thinking quite broadly about what a site is – not just an obvious forest, but also thinking about the broader infrastructures that might inform smart forests, and then looking at those sites in relation to a series of digital practices or operations from automation and optimization, to participation and datafication.

+ To follow up on the issue of governance, smart cities clearly benefit developers of technology, who are selling sensing technology to cities, so that they get the contracts for the upkeep and oversight of those networks. Is there any issue that you're thinking about when turning these public commons into something that's given over to private or corporate governance?

Yes, very much so. I'm interested in the ways in which smart cities have raised all of these issues in relation to who has responsibility for city governance and how it is increasingly becoming something that's undertaken by technology companies. More importantly, these same dynamics are mapping onto other environments, whether it's cities or forests, and how the forms of ownership, management, and governance are all shifting vis-à-vis digital technology.

These are classic questions of political ecology. These kinds of infrastructural arrangements aren't just material forms, they're also contractual and political. Forests have been looked at, to a large extent, as carbon sinks in various climate action plans. Forests could be preserved, for instance, in the Global South in order to offset carbon emissions in the Global North. There are planetary forms of governance, as part of climate change agreements, that are now being enacted, technologically and operationally, that could have even more significant political effects. This is something that a lot of technology companies are working on now, such as AI for Earth, and the idea of the Fourth Industrial Revolution. It's something that's very much at stake in the planetary responses to climate change.

+ Your book title *Program Earth: Environmental Sensing Technology and the Making of a Computational Planet* contains both the words "Earth" and "planet." Are they synonymous for you?

Yes and no. I wouldn't say they're exactly synonymous since there are many planets but only one Earth. However, I would very much want to avoid a kind of essentializing rhetoric that suggests that that one Earth is self-evident or universal. On this topic, I wrote a piece called *Becoming Planetary*, which works with Gayatri Chakravorty Spivak's notion of planetarity, which counteracts a universal approach to the planetary by thinking through certain kinds of relations and obligations that do not operate in the homogeneous space of the "global." I'm also starting a new short-monograph series, *Planetarities*, with some colleagues at Goldsmiths. We'll be including work that is experimental and textual, along with other practice-based ways of thinking through different formations of planetarities. Our hope is to open up new considerations and discussions around planetary governance, planetary politics, and to ask what is the planetary scale, and how might it be possible to develop different and more than just environmental inhabitations and politics in relation to the planetary?

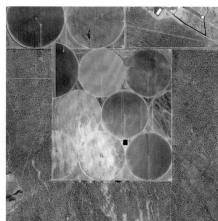
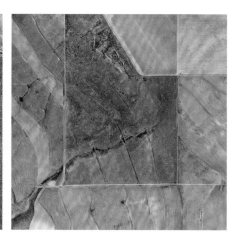

LUCY R. LIPPARD
WHAT ON EARTH?

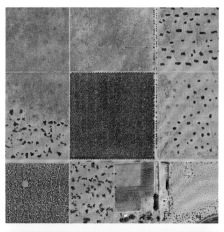
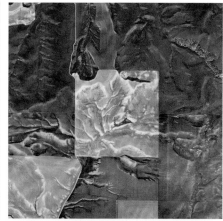
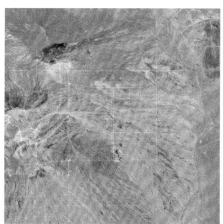

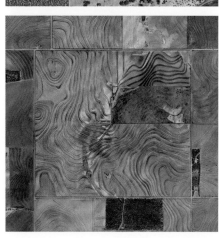

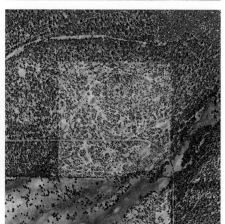

Lucy R. Lippard is a writer, activist, sometimes curator, and author of 25 books on contemporary art activism, feminism, place, photography, archaeology, and land use including *Undermining: A Wild Ride through Land Use, Politics and Art in the Changing West* (2014) and *Down Country: The Tano of the Galisteo Basin, 1250–1782* (2010). Co-founder of various activist artist groups, recipient of nine honorary degrees, a Guggenheim Fellowship, and other awards, she lives off the grid in rural New Mexico.

✚ ART CRITICISM, VISUAL ARTS, CULTURAL STUDIES

There is no better place from which to observe the geometry, geography, and geology of the planet than from a plane at several thousand feet. Glued to the window on a recent flight from New Mexico to Maine, I was struck by the designs below, inadvertently created by humanity through hard labor and greed, hope, and despair. It was a beautiful day, with cloud shadows racing across the land. The farther east we traveled the smaller were remnants of what we call wilderness – a bit depressing to a westerner accustomed to wider spaces. The sheer expanse of history and even geologic time is evoked as the land below us shifts and changes, as arid high desert and oil fields are replaced by wooded patches, as mountain ranges give way to plains, forests to farms, and streams to rivers (which sometimes resemble the historical roads they once were). Tiny dots dash along highways. Malls and subdivisions with an identical "variety" of architectural pastiche and curling culs-de-sac encroach on small farms. Scrawny third-growth forests await yet another clear cut. There are pits and there are erections, skyscrapers rising from the terrestrial origins of concrete. And finally there is the persistent sea, eating away at the Atlantic coastline. Personal landscape revelations, such as the incredibly labyrinthine coastline of Chesapeake Bay with its mansions, marinas, and industries suggest new narratives for the non-native that are hidden from limited views on the ground.

But where am I? Aside from the occasional comments of a chatty pilot, I have no idea. A pilot friend gave me a flight map, but it doesn't help much. The gap between print and fast-flowing visual experience is too wide. I have long wished for a streaming audio that would provide a map in real time as we careen over the continent.

Our cultural landscape can be parsed as a chart of political and financial power. Vast oil fields evoke outrage at the federal government's ongoing environmental deregulations. Miles of circle-irrigated agriculture in the desert raise questions of water supply and waste. But from this exalted viewpoint there is little hint of the climate chaos already evident to those whose heads are not in the sands of leisurely beaches and golf clubs.

This is not the iconic image of a "whole Earth," the lovely mottled marble seen from space. Despite the height from which I peer down, it is a series of amazingly intimate views, dreamlike in their rapid disappearance, comparable to lived experience and fleeting memories. The abstract expressionist painter Joan Mitchell once said, "I carry my landscape around with me." After spending a year in Devon, England, I found I could do the same, taking out-of-body hikes from Lower Manhattan across fields and hills and valleys that I once knew so well and were now so far away.

As a writer obsessed by place, flights are both fulfilling and frustrating. Haunted by the visible geometries and geographies and invisible geologies, I wonder if there is a way to fuse our patterned views from above and intimacy with known landscapes below. Would that help us non-professionals to understand more about landscape architecture at its roots, to learn the lessons of the bird's-eye-view? Scale presents an interesting problem. Miniaturization is too easy an answer, but landscape architects are equipped to conceptualize the fusion of aerial and ground views, and perhaps they will be crucial participants in public education around issues of climate disruption. ✚

Opposite: Landscapes across the United States. Images © Google (2019).

MAKING THE ROUGH

B.W. HIGMAN

B.W. Higman is emeritus professor of the Australian
National University and of the University of the West
Indies. He has doctorates in history and geography.
An Australian, he lived almost 30 years in Jamaica
and has published widely on Caribbean slavery and
landscape history. His work on the spatial concept
of flatness began with an interest in the Jamaican
lawn, spread to the flatness of the Australian
continent, and grew into an even larger project,
discussed in his book *Flatness* [2017].

✚ HISTORY, DESIGN, TECHNOLOGY

Crossing rough ground, in the absence of clearly defined
pathways, in unfamiliar territory, we choose our steps
carefully. Nature's landscape is unpredictable, the surface full
of hidden hazards: protruding rocks, sudden declivities, slippery
slopes, snakes in the grass. Its successful negotiation, indeed
our very survival, depends on close attention to navigational
clues, leaving us little time to appreciate the aesthetic qualities
of the larger landscape. When walking in a "landscaped" place, by
contrast, we expect few surprises, few risks to life and limb, and
feel able to lift our eyes to contemplate the world around us – or
safe to stare at the flat screens of our phones. We follow hard-
surfaced pathways built into the design and, most of us, obey
signs directing us away from the seductive softness of carpet-like
lawns: "keep off the grass!" If we trip on an unexpected upraised
paver in a public pathway, workers are dispatched to grind down
the offending stone, or we sue.

At the base of this contrast is flatness, a spatiality rarely found
in nature but essential to modern life. For many of us in today's
world, almost every surface on which we move, on most days,
is a flat engineered technology; our feet barely touch the rough
ground. Indeed, flatness is a concept and a condition central to the
entire architectural enterprise, and a key to many other aspects
of modernity. As an abstract concept, flatness is applied not only
in the physical work of engineering—moving earth and pouring
concrete—it is equally important in visualization and design, not
merely enabling simplified mental maps but also supplying the
tools and techniques needed to communicate ideas to clients,
and to satisfy surveyors, regulators, and lawyers.[1]

What is it about flatness that makes it so important and why
does it have a special place in the spatial history of the modern

GROUND PLANE

world? Broadly, the essence of flatness is invariance, a quality underpinning predictability and practicality, and contributing handsomely to profitability. In the modern world, flatness is valued for its reliable uniformity and relative lack of hazards, values that extend beyond the landscape to projects such as precision engineering and graphic design. These virtues spill over into concepts of social equality, justice, and fairness, exemplified by the level playing field. Yet flat landscape surfaces are often disparaged for their aesthetic blandness and baldness, their featurelessness, and indeed their emptiness.[2]

Negative perceptions of landscape flatness typically attach to broad vistas–deserts and plains–where topographic invariance can be viewed on a grand scale. These attitudes have something to do with the uncertainty of finding in such places the biodiversity needed to supply resources for survival, but also fears about getting lost in spaces lacking landmarks, going around in circles searching for waterholes or roadhouses. In contrast, local flatness is rarely disparaged or even noticed. In spite of these striking differences in landscape appreciation, one thing that is broadly common, whatever the scale, is a preference for pathways with surfaces as flat as possible to enable safe and speedy transit. Whether traveling through rocky mountains or across an arid plain, or simply negotiating a shopping mall, qualities of smoothness, straightness, and flatness are much to be desired. The modern engineered landscape caters effectively to these desires, ensuring efficiency and profit by constructing pathways that provide comfortable passage. Very often, these routes facilitate movement between diverse types of engineered sites–from home, to work, to shop–most of them, in turn, taking advantage of the profit to be made by building on a flat platform.

Focusing on movement and mobility offers a direct entry to analysis of the significance of flatness in landscape architecture, broadly defined, at all scales. It directs attention to the ways routes determine the flow of people–whether moving on foot, riding on animals, or driving wheeled vehicles–and to the impact on the landscape of these different modes of movement. Parallel to this flow of people is the movement of goods, often but not always sharing the same pathways and taking up increasingly large amounts of space. It is striking that wild animals also favor straight, flat routes so that, when roads or tracks are cut through forest, animals often use these as conduits, appreciating their practicality. However, pathways designed to suit human needs can have unintended consequences. Creating flat, direct routes may diminish protective natural barriers, channeling water into settlements. In addition to these physical and economic impacts, focusing on movement enables study of the ways travelers–locals and visitors–perceive and appreciate their surroundings. It also gives importance to the surfaces of routes–their shape, materials, textures–enabling an understanding of them as places in their own right (not non-places), essential elements of landscape. Broadly, then, movement brings to the fore both the aesthetic aspects of flatness and its fundamental practicality and profitability, and connects seemingly disparate landscapes and local ecologies.

The interaction between flatness and movement is important at every stage in the practice of landscape architecture, and has significance for the essential tools and techniques of the discipline. The process begins with visual flattening: the perception of flatness in the surfaces of existing topographies, and the evaluation and appreciation of such landscapes. What exactly it is that we see and whether our spatial images

constitute something "real"–out there, separate from our perception–is a question for neuroscience and philosophy, one that rarely keeps landscape architects awake at night. What should concern landscape architects, however, is the essential selectivity of our images and the ways they are complicated by relativities of time and motion. Visual awareness is fragmented and sequential. Rather than seeing landscapes as wholes, we pick and choose elements within the context of an abstract plane, flattened in the mind, and often unconsciously carried over into the design aspects of landscape architecture.[3]

Any transcription of the existing contents of a tract, whether large or small, is directed by an equivalent narrow focus–a flattening–determined both by perception and mission. The surveyor is always selective. For example, existing beaten paths, created by humans and animals, only sometimes leave clear visual traces and are therefore likely to be left off the plan. Equally significant, the representation of the elements within a tract of land, projected onto a sheet of paper, a canvas, or a flat screen, depends on the reduction of topographies to a two-dimensional state–making them plane–by means of cartography, painting and drawing, or photography.[4] The process is perhaps most obvious in the case of the world map, in which our picture of Earth has come to be constituted by a brutal assault on the spheroid – its surface distorted and misshapen, flattened out to fit a sheet of paper or flat screen.[5] Studies of landscape, from gardens to agroecology, geomorphology, and beyond, are rarely disturbed by the curvature of the Earth, and the principles are the same at all scales. Further, the warm embrace of GIS across a wide variety of fields and scales has ensured the longevity of cartographic flattening. Even when topography is represented by contour lines or perhaps 3-D

images, or displayed on a mobile wayfinding system, the final map or plan is presented on a flat surface.

Why are maps and plans flat? At base, the sheer overall practicality of flatness is a vital driver, facilitating the drawing of lines and enabling easy reproduction, enlargement, or reduction of efficiently stored plans. At another level, long before the invention of aerial photography, and working without surveying tools, human beings developed a capacity to picture the spatial relationships of landscape elements in their localities, and to transcribe these cognitive maps by drawing in (roughly flattened) sand or earth, just as they were able to draw (flattened) maps of the heavens. On the land, these abilities derived from long association with local topographies, known through the learning of wayfinding techniques and the linearity of routes. In walking or driving, it is most important to know where to turn and to look for landmarks and directional signs. Modern roads are littered with the latter but only occasionally refer to slope, as in "steep descent." The symbol ↑ says straight ahead not ascend. Public botanic gardens offer similar signage to guide visitors through the landscape. Maps and plans perform much the same purpose, though more difficult for many of us to follow. Thinking of the negotiable world as flat seems quite natural, whether designed or not, as well as being functional and efficient. Creating routeways that are themselves flat reinforces the practicality of the enterprise though not necessarily the aesthetic experience.

Moving on from the visualization and representation of flatness to the creative design of landscapes, there is no doubt that the adoption of new technologies has transformed the practice of drafting. Before electronic devices took over around 1990,

technical drawing rested firmly on flat working surfaces–drawing table, light table, and (tilted) drawing board–and employed many flat tools–protractor, set-square, T-square, straight-edge, celluloid curves–to draw on opaque or tracing paper. The drawing tools themselves–pens and pencils–were rarely flat but were guided by the edges of devices laid flat on the drawing board or table. Freehand drawing and lettering liberated the draftsperson from these devices but the surface of the plan remained unrelentingly flat. Alternatives were hard to imagine. Three-dimensional models were made but perhaps more for exhibition and marketing than used to work out a design.

Electronic devices and architectural software packages swiftly made much of the traditional hardware redundant, yet the fundamental flatness of the process of design proved resilient. Flat screens are stared at and tweaked, typically in a 2-D image; while virtual 3-D models through which users may be led from space to space tend to remain the domain of promoters, as with the old technology, rather than being seen as essential tools in drawing up designs. Although computers have vastly increased their speed and capacity to cope with big data since the 1970s, they largely perform the same functions as in those heady days. However, the development of holography and 3-D printing point in new directions, toward multidimensionality, away from flatness. So does the recent adoption of georeferenced building information modeling (BIM), in which digital data are embedded in multidimensional models, not amenable to printing on a flat surface.[6]

On the other hand, in some respects, there has been a recent step back toward flatness, notably in graphic design elements, in response to the proliferation of smaller devices that demand

simple graphics, often reflective of early 20th-century poster art with its undecorated flat patches of color. For some jobs, particularly those out of the ordinary, paper and pencil is recommended as the best starting point.[7] Software packages are criticized for imposing drawing tools that predetermine concepts of space rather than opening up ambiguities; in other words, flattening the infinite possibilities in design, and creating a Cartesian straightjacket for the designer. Perhaps the flat screen together with the often extreme flatness of computer-assisted graphics take on too much of the language of photography – once again with an eye to the glossy promotional image, encouraging a lively fightback by paper architects. What remains constant in this process of revolution and reaction is the steadfastness of the flat drawing surface, whatever the tools.[8]

Flatness is so essential to so many elements of the modern built environment that it is taken for granted. Thus it is not surprising that the ubiquity and persistence of flatness at every stage in the practice of landscape architecture–from the visualization and representation of existing landscapes to the drafting of new and renovated designs–builds on an unstated assumption that passages and pathways ultimately follow or float above an unseen foundational planar surface. In the landscape itself, beyond perception and imagination, the desire to make movement more efficient, profitable, and comfortable has been driven largely by wheeled devices, whether slow or fast. Wheels perform best on smooth surfaces and have limited tolerances to inclined slopes and sharp turns. The effect can be observed, for example, in the great lumbering harvesters that make their way slowly and steadily across laser-leveled croplands, and in high-speed trains from which travelers can barely catch sight of the surrounding landscape except for distant vistas. Laser-

levelers guide the blades of bulldozers; swatches of turfed grass are rolled out to create grassy carpets; concrete is poured and carefully smoothed and graded; pavers are set in sand to ensure the absence of risers waiting to trip the unwary walker; asphalt replaces cobbles finding its own liquid level. Roads, and their associated parking lots and domestic driveways, come to occupy significant areas, smothering the ground with concrete and tar, aggravating runoff, flattening and homogenizing everything in sight.[9] When eventually in the 21st century landscape architects began to think *unflattening* was the way forward, particularly to relieve the uniformity of urban passages, it proved problematic, partly because of the cost but also because of the necessity of predictable surfaces underfoot.

Although flattening has played a positive role in the transformation of landscapes, the negative aspects of planarity keep creeping back in. The greatly increased ease and speed of movement, and the profits generated by new transportation technologies, must be balanced against the perception of the sameness–indeed the flatness–of modern landscapes. This apparent contrast reflects not so much a paradox as an underappreciated association between the abstract and practical appeal of flatness and the context within which it flourished. It was the factories, machine tools, steam power, and railroads of the Industrial Revolution that engendered much of this development, and contributed in the longer term to climate change. It was flatness that provided the firm foundations for factory floors and demanded fossil fuels for rapid transit, thus transforming the landscape outside the satanic mills, as well as within their walls.[10]

Landscape flattening became even more vital with the dawn of the Anthropocene, a geological period generally thought to

commence around 1945, when for the first time humankind shifted more earth than was moved by nature.[11] Holes were dug and mounds raised up, but when it came to the construction of passages and pathways (and accompanying development) the typical goal of earthmoving was a flatter surface. However, the cutting of corridors and tunnels through steep land, to enable tolerably flat routes for motor vehicles and railroads, sometimes created conduits for the flow of water, enabling it to spread beyond existing physical barriers and creating level wetlands in times of flood. The experience is the same along coasts threatened by rising sea levels. Millions of people settled close to shorelines on flat "reclaimed" lands are now barely safe at high tide and becoming increasingly vulnerable to storm surges made more dangerous by the elevated temperature of warmed ocean surfaces. Sea level rise poses an even more dramatic threat—indeed an existential threat—to small, flat islands, condemned to a watery grave, hidden beneath the flat surface of the sea, their fate in part the ultimate outcome of global warming and the modern world's love affair with everything flat.

1 These themes are developed in B.W. Higman, *Flatness* (Reaktion Books, 2017).

2 Kamni Gill, "On Emptiness," *Journal of Landscape Architecture* 10, no. 2 (2015): 4–5.

3 Nick Chater, *The Mind is Flat: The Illusion of Mental Depth and the Improvised Mind* (Penguin Books, 2019), 39–46, 67; Graham Nerlich, *The Shape of Space* (Cambridge University Press, 1994), 263–68.

4 Christophe Schinckus, "Delimitation of Flatness in Painting," *Art and Perception* 6 (2018): 67–75.

5 John P. Snyder, *Flattening the Earth: Two Thousand Years of Map Projections* (University of Chicago Press, 1997).

6 Yannis Zavoleas & Mark Taylor, "From Cartesian to Topological Geometry: Challenging Flatness in Architecture," *Nexus Network Journal* 21 (2019): 5–18.

7 Elliot J. Gindis & Robert C. Kaebisch, *Up and Running with AutoCAD 2019: 2D Drafting and Design* (Academic Press, 2018), 549.

8 Sam Jacob, "Architecture Enters the Age of Post-Digital Drawing," *Metropolis*, 21 March 2017, https://www.metropolismag.com/architecture/architecture-enters-age-post-digital-drawing (accessed January 24, 2019).

9 John A. Jakle & Keith A. Sculle, *Lots of Parking: Land Use in a Car Culture* (University of Virginia Press, 2004); Christof Mauch & Thomas Zeller (eds), *The World Beyond the Windshield: Roads and Landscapes in the United States and Europe* (Ohio University Press, 2008); Francesca Russello Ammon, *Bulldozer: Demolition and Clearance of the Postwar Landscape* (Yale University Press, 2016).

10 Francis D. Klingender, *Art and the Industrial Revolution* (N. Carrington, 1947).

11 Roger LeB. Hooke, "On the History of Humans as Geomorphic Agents," *Geology* 28, no. 9 (2000): 843–46.

Aisling O'Carroll

RECONSTRUCTING THE

DENT DU REQUIN

Aisling O'Carroll is a registered landscape architect, trained in architecture and landscape architecture. Her work addresses relations between history, narrative, and representation in landscape, architecture, geology, and hybrids of the three, examining, in particular, critical approaches to reconstruction as design. She is currently completing her PhD at The Bartlett School of Architecture, UCL. Her work has been funded by UCL and the Landscape Research Group. She is co-founder and co-editor in chief of *The Site Magazine*.

✚ ARCHITECTURE, GEOLOGY, VISUAL ARTS

On July 20, 1872, French architect Eugène-Emmanuel Viollet-le-Duc set out at four o'clock in the morning from Montenvers in the French Alps and made his way over the Mer de Glace to an observation point at the base of the Tacul – the peak rising up at the confluence of the glaciers du Tacul and de Leschaux. He arrived just before eight o'clock in the morning and worked at the station undisturbed for the next seven hours.[1] Over the course of the day, he produced the *Vue panoramique de la station du Tacul* – a panoramic drawing recording the mountains that wrapped around him, stretching from La Tour Ronde in the south to Les Courtes in the north.[2] From where he stood, Mont Blanc lay hidden just behind the foregrounded ridges. On the left side of his view, between the Petit Rognon and the Aiguille de Blaitière, the particularly prismatic formation of an unnamed peak caught his attention. This formation (referred to by the architect simply as "l'envers de Blaitière" and known today as the Dent du Requin) subsequently became the subject of a striking analytical drawing exploring the architect's geometric rationalization of the granite mountain through an orthographic projection of the peak and its idealized form (image following pages).[3] This measured drawing offers a window into a historical conception of Earth's geophysical order and society's relationship with nature based on rational mathematical principles; it also reveals the limitations inherent in this deterministic ordering. Such historical constructions are useful to revisit when reconsidering our present relationship with nature as they shed light on the origins and influences that underpin and condition our current perceptions.

The question of society's relation to nature has been continually posed since its introduction in antiquity; however, it has become increasingly urgent over the last decade in the face of mounting pressure from intensifying global environmental change. In Western culture, the relationship has historically been presented through a dualistic framework that sets apart nature as something other than society. From biblical narratives to Romantic and Modernist thought, the Nature/Society dualism is heavily engrained in our perception of landscape.[4] Yet, we are presently being forced to reconsider this inherited dualism at a moment when, as environmental historian Jason Moore writes, "the flood of instability and change manifest in the allegedly separate domains of 'Nature' and 'Society' has become impossible to ignore."[5] While most design responses to today's instability are aimed at ameliorating or remedying identified crises–an ongoing and necessary effort–an alternative proposition suggests a more fundamental reframing of our perception of nature in order to enable radically new future engagements.[6] The work presented here proposes the reconstruction of past views of nature as a critical investigation of our present engagement with landscape in the context of climate change. Representations like Viollet-le-Duc's drawing of the Dent du Requin–"meaning-machines" in the words of scholar Donna Haraway–preserve and convey such historical constructions and the complex interactions that they represent.[7] The reconstruction of these past views helps to reveal the inherited, epistemic, and historical origins of our perception of nature and its limitations, and enables an expanded consideration of our present engagement.

Viollet-le-Duc's study of Mont Blanc spanned a series of eight annual expeditions made to the mountain between 1868 and 1876. This fieldwork led to his publication of a 300-page treatise on the mountain together with a 1:40,000 scale topographic map of the peak and its environs.[8] These two works presented the architect's summary of the mountain's history, its physical order, and the underlying principles of its structure and ongoing processes. While this geological focus at first appears to be a significant shift in the career of a well-established architect, he saw the geological investigation as an extension of his work begun in Gothic architecture, equating his study of ruined cathedrals to that of ruined peaks.[9] As he explained to an assembled party from the Société Géologique de France during an excursion to Brévent in 1875, the primitive form of Mont Blanc could be determined by following the same process as applied in the restoration of a monument.[10] In fact, Viollet-le-Duc began his geological investigation prior to his work in the Alps, developing his theory of a rational geological order in tandem with his rational ordering of architecture. In his article on "Style" published in volume eight of his *Dictionnaire raisonné de l'architecture française* two years before his first expedition to the Alps, he noted that the Earth's crust "is entirely in accordance with the laws of geometry" and explained that the rhombohedron was the basic geometric unit underlying its physical structure.[11] Evidence of his effort to draw out this geometric order can be found in the hundreds of drawings and sketches that he produced of the Mont Blanc massif. While many of his mountain sketches, such as his view of Mont Blanc

from the Aiguilles Rouges [image previous pages], recorded detailed "transcripts of nature," others clarified the idealized structure of the disintegrating peaks through simple strokes or pyramidal and rhombohedral volumes traced over the eroding landforms.[12] His didactic illustration of the Dent du Requin, however, offers the clearest and most complete rationalization of this order through the means of descriptive geometry.

In the drawing, two figures are placed side by side: on the left is a half-rhombohedron, the architect's universal, ideal geological form; and on the right, the ruin of the Dent du Requin. As Viollet-le-Duc described in a note scrawled in a corner of the sketch, the two figures depict the "crystalline system of the remnant peaks separating the glacier toward Blaitière from the Vallée Blanche."[13] The crystalline divisions are illustrated on the half-rhombohedron, delineating the measurable internal organization of the geological crust. By placing the two figures side by side, the drawing oscillates between the ideal model and the observed figure, between the action of restoration and that of ruination. The process of erosion is legible in the translation between the primitive form of the rhombohedron and the irregular form of the Dent du Requin, whose weathered profile reflects the structure of the rhombohedral matrix while displaying the complexities of the peak's own contingent history.[14]

As architectural historian Françoise Véry has noted in her discussion of the drawing and its idealized representation of the mountain, for Viollet-le-Duc the peak served as a synecdoche for the Earth, demonstrating the universality of the depicted geometric order and its underlying principles through extrapolation.[15] But beyond simply organizing the Earth's crust into a regular rhombohedral system, the drawing and its rationalization of geology reflects a particular reading of the Earth, history, and the relationship between society and nature. The idealization of nature and human's separation from it is evident in the representation through both the depiction of geology–conforming to mathematical perfection–as well as the projected point of view, constructed through a disembodied, aerial gaze that separates the viewer as an outside observer to the spectacle.[16] In this framework, the intellectual capacity of humans not only differentiates us but enables us to comprehend and cognitively control the rational, measurable order of nature.

As Haraway has demonstrated, knowledge (and in this case, scientific knowledge) is socially and historically constructed through the complex interactions of beings and objects and the stories that we tell of them.[17] Viollet-le-Duc's rational optic and dualistic separation was the result of his particular scientific imagination, as well as his historical context – including his social circles, his colleagues and teachers, synchronous developments in the arts and sciences, the sites and instruments of his research, and the specific geological phenomena that he observed. His rationalization of landform and geology was part of a larger attempt in the 18th and 19th centuries to provide a logically reasoned account for the history and structure of the Earth. In the nascent field of Earth sciences, the example of Newton's *Philosophiæ Naturalis Principia Mathematica* (1687), in which the entire cosmos was ordered by means of mathematical proofs, was held as the ultimate model through which to present an understanding of the Earth. The mathematical, inductive reasoning behind Viollet-le-Duc's interpretation of the Earth's crust follows this tradition, and his geometric idealization was not unprecedented. Twenty years earlier, the French geologist Élie de Beaumont, likely an acquaintance of Viollet-le-Duc, proposed an equally rigid geometric order for mountain chains at a planetary scale in his "réseau pentagonal."[18] While the studies by Viollet-le-Duc and de Beaumont stand out today for their rigid conformance to geometric principles and a Cartesian worldview, in the 19th-century context of scientific fields such as crystallography, their propositions fit within a broader fixation with the formal, geometric classification of natural systems and structures.[19]

In addition to establishing control and authority, these calculated, measurable systems were also concerned with aesthetics. This is particularly evident in Viollet-le-Duc's proposition, as he credited the "mathematical exactitude" of natural order with the production of the sublime, affective qualities of the mountains.[20] By analogizing his study of geology with that of architecture, he aligned the peak and geohistory with the aesthetic, historiographic reading of architectural monuments (Gothic architecture in particular). The use of orthographic projection offered him a measured visual language that provided the precision necessary for scientific reasoning and

1 Pierre A. Frey, "E. Viollet-Le-Duc, Itinéraire d'un Dessinateur," in *E. Viollet-Le-Duc et Le Massif Du Mont Blanc, 1868–1879* (Payot Lausanne, 1988), 27–30; Eugène-Emmanuel Viollet-le-Duc to Elisabeth (Tempier) Viollet-le-Duc, "Letter from Viollet-Le-Duc to His Wife," 22 July 1872, Médiathèque de l'architecture et du patrimoine.

2 Eugène-Emmanuel Viollet-le-Duc, *Vue panoramique de la station du Tacul* (20 July 1872), graphite, pencil, gouache, and watercolour on three joined pieces of paper, 30.1 cm x 137.9 cm, 20 July 1872, Médiathèque de l'architecture et du patrimoine.

3 Although the sketch is left undated and the peak identified only as "the remnant peaks separating the glacier towards Blaitière from the Vallée Blanche," I have determined from archival and topographic research that the illustrated peak is the Dent du Requin. I established the timeline and origin of the orthographic sketch by reviewing the itineraries of Viollet-le-Duc's Mont Blanc expeditions as well as his visual and written descriptions of the peak. The hike to the Tacul in 1872 was the first (and likely only) time that he reached a position to observe the Dent du Requin, and thus, his panoramic sketch from July 20 records the only view that served as basis for his reconstruction. For a description of "l'envers de Blaitière," see: Eugène-Emmanuel Viollet-le-Duc, *Le Massif Du Mont-Blanc. Étude Sur Sa Construction Géodésique et Géologique, Sur Ses Transformations, et Sur l'état Ancien et Moderne de Ses Glaciers* (Jean Baudry, 1876), 60–61.

4 "Landscape" in the inclusive sense of the geographical and the worked ground as well as the pictorial and cultural interpretations.

5 Jason W. Moore, *Capitalism in the Web of Life: Ecology and the Accumulation of Capital* (Verso, 2015), 13.

6 See James Graham's work for an example of a similar approach addressing the question of climate, in particular, "Climatic Imaginaries," in James Graham et al. (eds), *Climates: Architecture and the Planetary Imaginary* (Columbia Books on Architecture and the City, Lars Müller Publisher, 2016), 9–14.

7 Donna Haraway, "Teddy Bear Patriarchy: Taxidermy in the Garden of Eden, New York City, 1908–1936," *Social Text* 11 (Winter, 1984–1985): 52.

8 Viollet-le-Duc, Le Massif Du Mont-Blanc; Eugène-Emmanuel Viollet-le-Duc, *Le Massif Du Mont Blanc. Carte Dressée à 1:40,000, Par E. Viollet-Le-Duc, d'après Ses Relevés et Études Sur Le Terrain de 1868 à 1875, Avec l'aide Des Minutes Du Dépôt Topographique de La Guerre et Des Levés de M. Mieulet.*, 1:40,000 (Paris, 1876).

9 Viollet-le-Duc states: "To analyze carefully a group of mountains, the manner in which they were formed, and the causes of their ruin...is to devote oneself to a work of methodical analysis which is, on a grander scale, analogous to that to which the practical architect and the archaeologist applies himself when drawing conclusions from the study of buildings." In Eugène-Emmanuel Viollet-le-Duc, *Mont Blanc: A Treatise on Its Geodesical and Geological Constitution; Its Transformations; and the Ancient and Recent State of Its Glaciers*, trans. Benjamin Bucknall

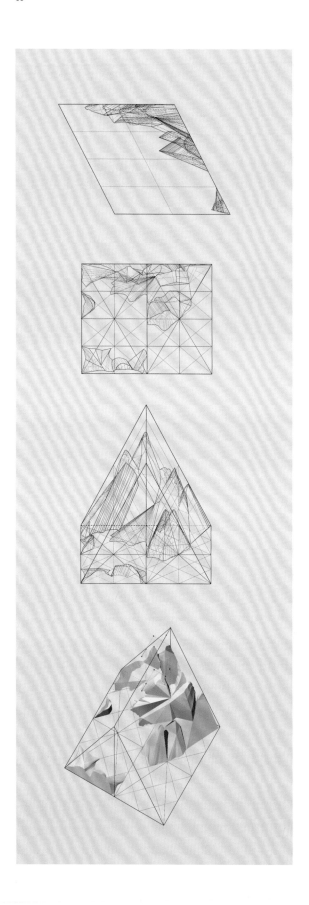

speculation while avoiding mimetic representation.[21] Although he used this measured projection to ensure objectivity, like any scientific visualization, the representation inevitably entailed the wedding of aesthetic and scientific concerns. His artistic ability and profuse drawing production set his practice apart from his contemporaries in the Earth sciences. He developed his ideas through drawing before writing, generating a richly illustrated body of work and a thoroughly visualized construction of geology – one that lends itself to reconstruction, as demonstrated in the drawings shown here.

The actual Dent du Requin is surrounded on three sides by glaciers. The peak erupts from this icy landscape, rising sharply toward the west with its highest point leading toward the Aiguille du Plan. On its east face, eroded layers of parallel granite beds create a series of ridges stepping down to the base of the peak. The overall form lends itself to a prismatic reading, particularly when viewed from the northeast, as Viollet-le-Duc observed it in the summer of 1872. From this limited perspective, recorded in his 1872 panoramic drawing, the architect extrapolated his depiction of the peak's crystalline system by carrying out two translations. Firstly, he translated the peak into a parallel, orthographic projection, a distortion of the human eye's perspectival vision. And secondly, he shifted the viewing angle to an aerial vantage impossible to attain from anywhere on the ground. The result is an entirely constructed view, relying on mathematical calculation and interpolation. Viollet-le-Duc's expertise in descriptive geometry enabled him to work in this manner, as he said himself, "a long habit of drawing objects on the spot and deducing their geometric form through a series of perspective effects facilitated me, moreover, in this type of work."[22]

Viollet-le-Duc carefully plotted the base of the peak, the edge where the stone breaks through the snow and ice, against the crystalline divisions of the rhombohedron's oblique central plane, demonstrating the coherence he found between the two systems. The existing peak floats on the page, sliced at its base and abstracted from the rest of the mountain. It is anchored only by the geometry of the rhombohedral prism and yet it remains recognizable as the peak originally drawn in his panorama. Above the base, the mass of the landform rises as six distinct peaks extending vertically into the volume of the rhombohedron. The assembly appears plausible (if fantastic) at first glance; however, upon closer inspection it is evident that there is an impossible alignment within the sketched peak.

As drawn, the Dent du Requin appears to be perfectly circumscribed by the form of the rhombohedron, when in fact the elevated peaks cannot correspond to their plotted base while fitting within the geometric volume. This misalignment is most clearly evident in the top left corner of the projection where the base of the peak lands just shy of the back edge of the rhombohedral plane, while above it, vertical peaks stand two layers deep, occupying a depth much greater than that remaining between the base of the peak and the vertical face of the rhombohedron. The apparent coherence of the idealized form and observed ruin is only possible by means of visual trickery in a convincingly drawn projection. The incongruity of the two is concealed behind the appearance of mathematical truth. Through the process of reconstructing Viollet-le-Duc's illustration, the limitations and errors of his construction become apparent. In his attempt to be faithful to a purely scientific mode, he inadvertently demonstrated the incapacity of such a rational framework to accommodate the complex reality of the geological monument. While mathematics was (and generally is) trusted as an unbending, irreducible truth, Viollet-le-Duc's geometric rationalization of the peak required an additional element of imagination that is unacknowledged and hidden in the orthographic projection of his drawing.

In my own study (images opposite and following pages), the illustration is reconstructed by projecting the architect's linework into three-dimensional space, perpendicular to the original drawing's surface. The form of the peak is modeled within this array of projected lines, in the space where they intersect the rhombohedral prism, and adapted to correspond with the original drawing. The reconstructions use hybrid analogue and digital methods and follow a process informed by Viollet-le-Duc's drawing techniques. These new meaning-machines deconstruct Viollet-le-Duc's rationalization of geology by reconstructing both the peak and the relationship between observer and monument. The process of reconstruction, however objectively it is intended, is not only scientific but necessarily speculative, and in reconstructing Viollet-le-Duc's Dent du Requin, the work inevitably generates something new (for a second time around).

In the century and a half since Viollet-le-Duc's work, we have largely moved away from the paradigm of geometrical formalism that structured his (and many of his colleagues' and forebears') reading of the Earth's geophysical systems. Nonetheless, the Nature/Society dualism and preoccupation with calculation that underpinned his methods continues to shape our present engagement with nature. Today, this interest has shifted toward an emphasis on the collection of increasingly precise data to survey landform and measure change, quantify ecological valuation, delineate geopolitical boundaries, and qualify geophysical characteristics, for example. In the context of climate change, the fixation with measurement continues as an effort to procure control through knowledge, but it also remains intimately tied to affective experience as well, both in the emotional impression of the phenomena quantified and in the response triggered by the data itself and its implications. Recognizing and supporting the importance and centrality of scientific work to our present understanding of natural systems, this work proposes a historiographic approach–through reconstruction– to critically reframe the way we interpret and respond to such information and to expand our present and future engagement with landscapes and natures. Rather than perpetuating the inherited Nature/Society dualism, this approach recognizes that any perceived relationship between nature and society is

(Sampson Low, Marston, Searle & Rivington, 1877), 12–13.

10 Alphonse Favre, "Compte-Rendu de l'excursion Du 6 Septembre Au Brévent," *Bulletin de La Société Géologique de France* 3, no. 3 (1875): 793–94.

11 Eugène-Emmanuel Viollet-le-Duc, "Style," in *The Foundations of Architecture: Selections from the Dictionnaire raisonné,* trans. Kenneth D. Whitehead (George Braziller, 1990), 237–40.

12 Charles Wethered, "Viollet-Le-Duc: A Further Sketch of his Life and Works," *Transactions of the Royal Institute of British Architects* IV (1888): 63.

13 Annotations translated from Viollet-le-Duc's drawing of the Dent du Requin.

14 As architectural historian Martin Bressani notes, the degradation of the landscape was necessary to Viollet-le-Duc's interpretation of its systematic order, "(the) very process of ruination is what best reveals the crystalline system," in Martin Bressani, "Eugène Viollet-Le-Duc," *Drawing Matter* (blog), 7 February 2017, https://www.drawingmatter. org/sets/drawing-week/martin-bressani-eug%C3%A8ne-viollet-le-duc/.

15 Françoise Véry, "Àpropos d'un Dessin de Viollet Le-Duc," in Pierre A. Frey (ed.), *E. Viollet-Le-Duc et Le Massif Du Mont-Blanc, 1868-1879* (Payot Lausanne, 1988), 113.

16 See Thordis Arrhenius' writing on Viollet-le-Duc for further discussion of his use of the "disembodied eye" in his rationalization and abstraction of both landscape and architectural systems: Thordis Arrhenius, The Fragile Monument: On Conservation and Modernity (Black Dog Publisher, 2012), 81–83. In Viollet-le-Duc's architectural novella, Learning to Draw, one of the main characters, M. Marjorin, explains that humans are distinguished from all other animals by the superior quality of intelligence: Eugène-Emmanuel Viollet-le-Duc, Learning to Draw; or The Story of a Young Designer, trans. Virginia Champlin (G.P. Putnam's Sons, 1888), 211–12.

17 Haraway, "Teddy Bear Patriarchy," 52–53.

18 Élie de Beaumont, *Notice Sur Les Systèmes de Montagnes*, 3 vols (P. Bertrand, 1852). While travelling in the Pyrenees in 1833, Viollet-le-Duc spent several days in the company of a "M. É de Beaumont," who is believed to have been the geologist Élie de Beaumont. Eugène-Emmanuel Viollet-le-Duc, *Voyage Aux Pyrénées*, 1833 (Les Amis du Musée Pyrénéen, 1972); Armand Brulhart-Danna, "La Carte Du Massif Du Mont-Blanc de Viollet-Le-Duc, 1876," in Frey (ed.), *E. Viollet-Le-Duc et Le Massif Du Mont-Blanc*, 42.

19 See Laurent Baridon's discussion of crystallography in relation to Viollet-le-Duc's practice in Laurent Baridon, L'imaginaire Scientifique de Viollet-Le-Duc, Villes, Histoires, Culture, Société (Éditions L'Harmattan, 1996), 119–24.

20 Viollet-le-Duc, "Style," 236, 240; Eugène Emmanuel Viollet-le-Duc, "Lecture I," in *Discourses on Architecture*, trans. Benjamin Bucknall, vol. 1 (George Allen & Unwin Ltd., 1860), 18–20.

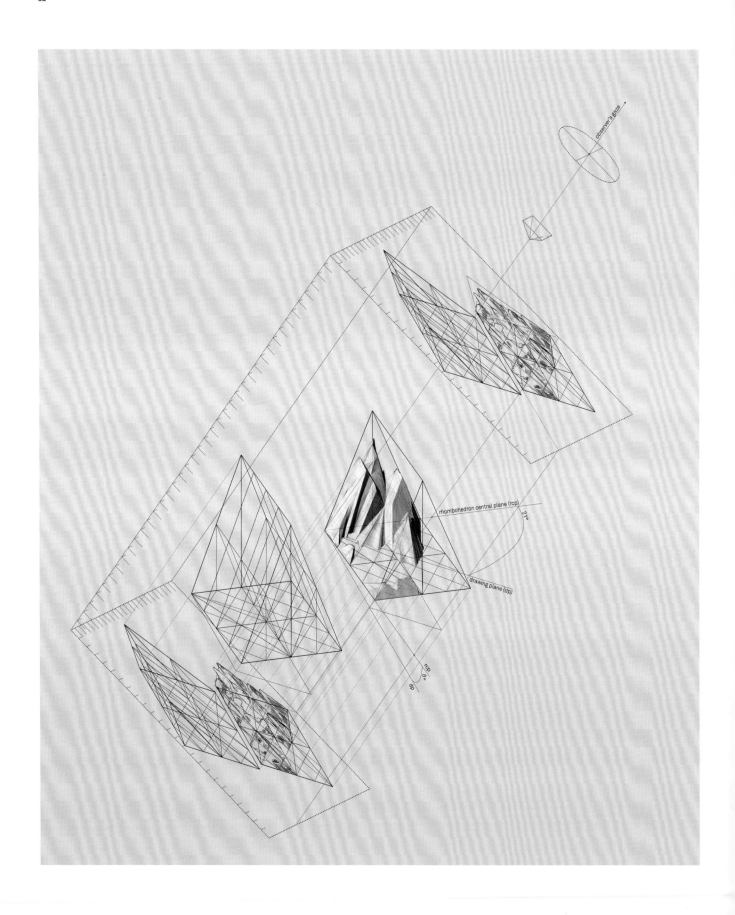

observer's gaze

rhombohedron central plane (rcp)

27°

drawing plane (dp)

rcp

5°

dp

principally historical and instead works to reveal the social and historical construction of such relationships and knowledge through their preserved representations (meaning-machines). Demonstrated through the reconstruction of Viollet-le-Duc's Dent du Requin, historiographic work can reveal the role that society, history, and even imagination plays in constructing our ways of seeing and thinking.

As Moore notes, the question of the relationship between society and nature "cannot be answered in a dualist frame," rather, it requires a historical method that in turn implies a radical new praxis.[23] The construction (and reconstruction) of history goes beyond historical analysis and is inevitably a creative project. Demonstrated in Viollet-le-Duc's practice, as well as in more recent work including that of Haraway and Moore, historiographic work has the capacity to transform methods, practices, and ways of seeing in the present. As Moore writes, "How we tell stories of the past and how we respond to challenges of the present, are intimately linked."[24] At a moment of increasing environmental instability, while we cannot escape our own participation in the cycle of knowledge's social construction, this historical reconstruction offers a tool to radically reframe how we approach, engage, respond to, and design with changing natural systems. Indeed, while critiquing the rationalization of geology in his construction, this research simultaneously draws on Viollet-le-Duc's practice of design through reconstruction—his own continually relevant words are strikingly similar to Moore's more recent ones quoted above: "The retrospective work being carried out today also relates to future problems and will provide help in facilitating the solutions of such problems. Synthesis follows analysis."[25] Recognizing the historicity of our relationship with (and construction of) nature is critical to reconsidering our future relations. Returning to Haraway, deciphering the construction of each of these "time slices" is necessary to understanding how past relations continue to shape the present.[26] The process is akin to reconstructing each strata in the archaeology of our perception of nature in order to expand the consideration of our possible futures.

21 Bruno Latour and Samuel Edgerton describe the critical role that perspectival projection played in the development of objective, transportable scientific communication, while Martin Rudwick provides an account of the integral role that visual language played in the development of geological science, in Bruno Latour, "Visualisation and Cognition: Drawing Things Together," *Knowledge and Society Studies in the Sociology of Culture Past and Present*, vol. 6 (Jai Press, 1986), 7–9; Samuel Y. Edgerton, "The Renaissance Artist as Qualifier," in *The Perception of Pictures*, vol. 1, Academic Press Series in Cognition and Perception (Academic Press, Inc, 1980), 180–85; Martin J. S. Rudwick, *Bursting the Limits of Time: The Reconstruction of Geohistory in the Age of Revolution* (The University of Chicago Press, 2005), 75–80; Martin J. S. Rudwick, "The Emergence of a Visual Language for Geological Science 1760–1840," *History of Science* 14 (1976): 149–95.

22 Viollet-le-Duc made this comment to the Société de Géographie while describing his method in the analogous exercise of translating perspective views into a planimetric survey for his topographic map of Mont Blanc: Eugène-Emmanuel Viollet-le-Duc, "Nouvelle Carte Topographique Du Massif Du Mont Blanc," *Bulletin de La Société de Géographie* 8 (December 1874): 44.

23 Moore, *Capitalism in the Web of Life*, 33–34.

24 Ibid., 17.

25 Eugène-Emmanuel Viollet-le-Duc, "Restoration," in *The Foundations of Architecture: Selections from the Dictionnaire Raisonné*, trans. Kenneth D. Whitehead (George Braziller, 1990), 198.

26 Haraway, "Teddy Bear Patriarchy," 52.

NOAH HERINGMAN

THE ROCKS MUST BE STRANGE

Noah Heringman teaches English at the University of Missouri. His publications include *Romantic Rocks, Aesthetic Geology* (2004); *Sciences of Antiquity: Romantic Antiquarianism, Natural History, and Knowledge Work* (2013); and a digital edition of *Vetusta Monumenta* (2019). He is currently completing a monograph entitled *Deep Time: A History*.

✚ HISTORY, LITERATURE, DESIGN, GEOLOGY

Opposite: Artificial volcano at Dessau-Wörlitz's Island of Stone mid-eruption.

Following: "The Stone of Wörlitz," aquatint by Wilhelm Friedrich Schlotterbeck after Carl Kuntz (1797).

Thanks to the efforts of gifted popular science writers such as John McPhee and Robert McFarlane, deep time is widely held to be synonymous with geological time. Many writings on the Anthropocene epoch presuppose this association, since the idea of a human-driven Earth system effects a spectacular collapse of historical into geological time. There are other deep-water currents in the time stream, however, and some of these have been mapped by ethnographers, literary critics, and science fiction writers including J.G. Ballard (*The Drowned World*) and Eric Temple Bell, who revisits the "illimitable desert" of the primitive world only to uncover an even deeper past of advanced civilizations fueled by limitless energy in *The Time Stream* (1931).[1] Geological evidence suggests that the original, molten earth formed about 4.6 billion years ago, but this period is only about a *kalpa* in Hindu cosmology, a single day in the life of Brahma. Since Brahma is now about 50 years old, this makes our current world much older, well over 150 trillion years.[2]

Deep time is older than geology, and cross-cultural speculation about rocks and time merits renewed attention as a pursuit that informed the creation of the modern geological time scale. Even the *Dissertation on Oriental Gardening* (1772), a seemingly frivolous exercise in *chinoiserie* by the Georgian architect Sir William Chambers (1723–1796), has something new to offer a world in which geological "scenes of terror" are envisioned in earnest by spectators haunted by global warming and the catastrophic depletion of natural resources. Though blatantly inauthentic in many of its details, Chambers's account of Chinese landscape design offers a distorted echo of Chinese practice in its treatment of rocks, as suggested by the following injunction to designers of gardens in a late Ming treatise: "At the foot of the pine tree are rocks and the rocks must be strange."[3] The most extravagant "scenes of terror" in Chambers's imagined Chinese garden feature

not only "impending barren rocks" and "dark caverns," but even artificial volcanoes set in real mountaintops.

In a geological context, strange and terrifying rocks are more than just aesthetic convention. The creators of Western geology also looked to the East in their search for a new chronology more consistent with the testimony of the rocks. Georges Cuvier, in setting up paleontology as the means for establishing a clear succession of geological "revolutions" prior to human history, conjures up the extraordinary scale of some non-Western cosmologies by referencing the *Mahabharata*, though he quickly dismisses it as "nothing more than a poem." Johann Gottfried Herder takes Eastern cosmologies more seriously, finding geological origin stories in Hindu myth and effectively conflating oral traditions with geological time by placing them outside chronology.[4] Both Cuvier and Herder were influenced by the natural history of Georges-Louis Leclerc, Comte de Buffon, whose *Epochs of Nature* (1778) proposed a geochronology of 75,000 years – revolutionary for its time. Buffon adduced geological evidence for his theory that human antiquity also predated established chronology and could be traced to central Asia. In his history of cosmic time, Hans Blumenberg has pointed out that for these Enlightenment thinkers, embedded in European colonialism, the embrace of non-Western perspectives and radically expanded cosmologies did not (yet) contradict their anthropocentrism or

their Eurocentric view of progress.[5] Nonetheless, the path to a naturalistic understanding of time lay through cross-cultural encounter, as became ever clearer in the series of scientific voyages leading up to Charles Darwin's voyage on the *Beagle*.

If the "abyss of time" was not yet a source of existential terror in the stark rocky landscapes envisioned by Chambers, there is something else at stake in them besides the sublime in its then-popular Burkean form.[6] Chambers recognized that rocks could be strange to the point of terror. In recommending that garden designers render their rocks as terrible as possible, Chambers is taking his cue from ideas of the sublime that were popular with tourists and philosophers, but is also drawing on his own experience in China. The sublime can be an alibi for imperial control, as noted by Chambers's critics then and now. But the strangeness and terror of Chambers's rocky spectacles is not altogether staged. These scenes are genuinely haunted by the expanding geological time scale, on the one hand, and the threat of resource exhaustion, on the other. Chambers's landscape theory speaks to these fears by imagining China as the source of an alternative tradition concerning time and antiquity and as a vast fund of resources yet to be tapped by the burgeoning British Empire.

Although it has now been rejected by the Anthropocene Working Group, Paul Crutzen's proposed dating of the epoch to 1784–the year that James Watt's steam engine was perfected for industrial application–still makes sense when considering the industrial and postindustrial modernity first incorporated into the theory of garden design by Chambers and continued into the present through a variety of landscape traditions. Although situated in scenes of terror "bear[ing] every mark of depopulation," behind the scenes Chambers's artificial volcanoes were converting mineral resources into consumer goods:

> [T]o add to both the horror and sublimity of these scenes, they sometimes conceal in cavities, on the summits of the highest mountains, founderies, lime-kilns, and glass-works; which send forth large volumes of flame, and continued columns of thick smoke, that give to these mountains the appearance of volcanoes.[7]

Along with the pagoda at Kew Gardens, there is an artificial volcano in the ducal gardens at Dessau-Wörlitz [1794], one of the numerous continental *jardins anglo-chinois* inspired by Chambers's writings and built works that preserves his legacy as a landscape architect. This volcano, Der Stein, is on a more modest scale and produces no iron or glass, but eruptions are still staged there on special occasions. What is missing from this domesticated version is the setting of "impending barren rocks," supporting nothing but "brushwood and brambles." There is little here to differentiate the preindustrial or prehuman landscape of barren rocks from the postindustrial landscape of depletion; the industrial component of Chambers's "scene of terror" conflates those two temporalities. Underscoring this conflation, the historian Fredrik Albritton Jonsson has argued that resource exhaustion was merely deferred by the development of industrial capitalism because it allowed more-efficient exploitation of dwindling resources.[8] Industrial modes of extraction were welcomed for this reason, as Jonsson shows, by 18th-century observers who were already confronted by deforested, depleted landscapes and catastrophic migrations.

In this way, desolate rocky landscapes may be seen to figure the eclipse of human history [or "depopulation"] as a prospect associated with prehuman time even before there was anything like a geological time scale properly speaking. The Anthropocene debate, taking its cue in a loose sense from Earth system science, has fostered renewed artistic engagement with barren and depleted landscapes and the cultural and economic fears associated with them. DESIGN EARTH, also featured in this issue of *LA+*, has produced works in this category, including *After Oil, Of Oil and Ice*, and *Georama of Trash*. Neyran Turan's *Museum of Lost Volumes* visually assumes the conjectural post-climate-change vantage point also associated with much Anthropocene writing. Edward Burtynsky's photography, and his collaborative Anthropocene Project specifically, might also be cited here as documenting depleted landscapes and impending resource exhaustion. As the poet Amy De'Ath observes in her critique of Burtynsky, however, the humanist framework of the sublime collapses under the alien pressure of these inorganic landscapes. De'Ath

repudiates the claim to sublimity that these images seem to advance: "fuck you negative sublime / ah you toxic sublime / fuck you technological sublime / ah you inverted sublime / fuck you industrial sublime."[9]

Chambers, too, is sometimes critiqued as a purveyor of the industrial or technological sublime, and of Orientalism, but too exclusive an emphasis on what Chambers himself called "the garb of fiction" obscures the real grounds for the strangeness and terror that he attributes to rocks in his polemical account of the Chinese garden. Chambers visited China three times while he was in the service of the Swedish East India Company in the 1740s and began advising Prince Frederick on Chinese buildings for Kew as early as 1749. His *Designs for Chinese Buildings* followed in 1757 and this program culminated with his construction of the pagoda there, documented in the published set of plans and elevations [image following page, 1763], in which Chambers declared of Kew, "That which was once a Desart is now an Eden."[10] Just as this work was driven more by the European fashion of *chinoiserie* than by an aim of authenticity, so too the *Dissertation* used Chinese aesthetics in the subsidiary role of a "mask" to disguise Chambers's polemic against the pseudo-natural garden designs of Lancelot "Capability" Brown. Further, European traders were strictly confined to the foreigners' quarter in Canton until well into the 19th century, and it is unclear how much Chambers would have seen of authentic Chinese gardens.[11] Nonetheless, audiences expected some degree of authenticity from an architect who had the rare experience of visiting China, and some possible Chinese influences shine through his manifest intention of using a Chinese "mask." Chen Jiru's dictum, "the rocks must be strange," provided our first illustration.

Scholarship on traditional Chinese gardens suggests that the fantastic, literary streak is precisely what Chambers shares with 17th-century Chinese garden theorists. Stanislaus Fung challenges the primarily Western scholarly tradition of reading Chinese works on gardens as factual descriptions, showing that "in the many discussions of *Yuan ye* [Ji Cheng's *The Figuration of Gardens*]...a literal reading of semantic content has obscured the gestural and performative aspects of the treatise."[12] The resemblance between Chambers's descriptions and those of Cao Xueqin, in *The Story of the Stone* [1763], provides another index of their literary plausibility. He could not have known the *Story of the Stone* and its garden descriptions, but their similarity to his suggests that he had some access, if not to Chinese gardens, then to accounts like those the novel draws on. Cao's gardens are abundantly stocked with artificial hills, rocks, and ravines, a miniature farm, and other properties mentioned by Chambers.[13] Chambers's obvious plagiarizing of Western sources on China is no argument against the influence of his own experience there. Magnus Olausson has shown that he was already a keen student of architecture while traveling for the Swedish East India Company; the virtual quarantine

of the merchant "factories" in Canton, relieved by glimpses of half-imagined bounty and magnificence, can only have been a formative experience.[14]

The distorted echo of Chinese practice, and of canonical Chinese literature on gardens, helps to defamiliarize the aesthetic conventions of the sublime. Sitting slightly askew in Chambers's fantastic landscapes, *chinoiserie* and the sublime here betray an instability in Enlightenment thinking about the Earth and time, a shadow of continuity that is never quite extinguished by the strict separation between natural and human history attributed to the Enlightenment in Dipesh Chakrabarty's influential account.[15] Beginning with a defense of the high status of Chinese landscape designers as intellectuals and philosophers, Chambers injects a new self-consciousness about raw materials into a traditional trope in English writing about gardens that dates back to Sir William Temple's *Upon the Gardens of Epicurus* (1680). His intervention into contemporary aesthetic debate about the landscape garden borrows heavily from Thomas Whately's *Observations on Modern Gardening* (1770), a more practical approach structured around raw materials, with long chapters on ground, wood, water, and of course rocks. Chambers, with his technical focus on artificial rocks and volcanoes, evokes the tradition of applied science deriving

from the Jesuits' reports from China, which speculated on the economic viability of Chinese arts and manufactures in the West.[16] Chambers's cross-cultural approach to landscape situates this early industrial attitude in a global context.

Chambers's vision of rocks shares its strangeness with the visions of naturalists from the same period who looked into the abyss of time and found an abundance of fossil fuels seemingly as inexhaustible as the profound annals of prehuman history. The most spectacular case of this delusion occurs in Buffon's *Epochs of Nature*, the first complete English translation of which was not published until 2018. The more human beings multiply, the more they will have "recourse to these immense deposits of combustible matter," he predicts; but these are so ancient, and so vast, that "they will never exhaust them."[17] Precisely because it is not a scientific text, Chambers's *Dissertation* allows us to keep in view the strangeness that Europeans attributed to other cultures as a precondition for the emergence of geological time as such. The rocks in designed landscapes manifest this cultural legacy by staging the radical discontinuity between geology and history, both as exoticizing fantasy and as a more or less aestheticized reckoning with inhuman time.

In a supposed apology for the extravagance of his *Dissertation*, Chambers returns again to "forges, collieries, mines, coal tracts, brick or lime kilns, glass-works, and different objects of the horrid kind" as properties that "compleat the aspect of desolation" in a designed landscape.[18] His appropriation of the Chinese garden compensates for the lack of European access to the commodities of a culture then most impervious to colonial expansion, as confirmed by the failure of Lord Macartney's 1793 mission to improve conditions for trade. Yet Chambers's fiction of imperial control alternates between superabundance and scarcity, suggesting that the untapped wealth of China may be needed to stave off resource exhaustion.

However egregious its Orientalism, Chambers's *Dissertation* has nothing of the xenophobia and race hatred of *The Time Stream*, published by Bell, a distinguished American mathematician, under the pseudonym John Taine. Taine's vision of an ancient eugenic science that has thousands of generations worth of genetic records at its fingertips transcends the scale of human history to posit an alternative, Hellenized version of human origins rather than a deep prehuman past for the Earth itself. *The Time Stream* is relevant here, nonetheless, as an inspiration for Robert Smithson's *Spiral Jetty* (1970), a designed landscape on the larger scale of land art. Taine's "time stream" flows in a circle, deviating from the linear model of time ("time's arrow") and, more subtly, from the cyclical model of time as well. Smithson reads passages from the novel toward the end of his film *The Spiral Jetty* that allude to the form of the spiral nebula, linked to the distinctive forms of energy and time that Bell envisions. At the same time, Smithson's spiral anticipates one of the most common graphic representations of the Geological Time Scale in recent decades. The spiral uses rocks to capture the strangeness of time, evoking a kind of terror made vivid by

Smithson in his essay "The Spiral Jetty." "These fragments of a timeless geology laugh without mirth at the time-filled hopes of ecology."[19] The film shows us bulldozers and dump trucks at work, piling basalt and limestone bedrock onto the spiral.

Given enough bulldozers, Chambers might have realized his dream of siting a glassworks inside a hollowed-out mountaintop to perfect his "scene of terror." A motorcycle in the desert is the preferred artmaking tool of Reno, a fictional female avatar or permutation of Smithson in Rachel Kushner's novel *The Flamethrowers* (2013), classified by the critic Kate Marshall as a defining novel of the Anthropocene. As the geological footprint of industrial and postindustrial societies has expanded in scale, the discourse of landscape has magnified the concern over human inscription in the rock record and, increasingly, the anxiety over any potential legibility of that trace in the future. Meditations on the unforgiving nature of rock have a longer history. In this context, Chambers's idea of Chinese landscape aesthetics is remarkable not only for its global reach but also for its recognition of resource exhaustion and historical decline as a logical possibility in the midst of empire and superabundance.

1 See John McPhee, *Annals of the Former World* (Farrar, Straus, Giroux, 1998); Robert McFarlane, *Underland: A Deep Time Journey* (Hamish Hamilton, 2019); J.G. Ballard, *The Drowned World* (1962; Liveright, 2012); and "John Taine" (E. T. Bell], *The Time Stream* (rpt. Garland, 1975), 15.

2 W. Randolph Kloetzli, "Myriad Concerns: Indian Macro-Time Intervals ("Yugas," "Sandhyas," and "Kalpas") as Systems of Number," *Journal of Indian Philosophy* 41, no. 6 (December 2013): 631–53. See also Meena Nayak, "Cycles of Great Time," *The Blue Lotus: Myths and Folktales of India* (Aleph, 2018), 507–8.

3 William Chambers, *Dissertation on Oriental Gardening* (rpt. London: Gregg, 1972), 37; Chen Jiru, "On One's Place of Dwelling," quoted in John Minford, "The Chinese Garden: Death of a Symbol," *Studies in the History of Gardens and Designed Landscapes* 18, no. 3 (1998): 3, 257.

4 Georges Cuvier, "Discourse préliminaire," *Recherches sur les ossemens fossiles des quadrupèdes* (Deterville, 1812), vol. I, p. 101; Herder, *Ideen zur Philosophie der Geschichte der Menschheit*, ed. Martin Bollacher (Deutscher Klassiker Verlag, 1989), 400.

5 Georges-Louis Leclerc, Comte de Buffon, *Epochs of Nature*, ed. and trans. Jan Zalasiewicz, Anne-Sophie Milon & Mateusz Zalasiewicz (University of Chicago Press, 2018), xxvi; Blumenberg, *Lebenszeit und Weltzeit* (Suhrkamp, 1986), 224.

6 Edmund Burke, *A Philosophical Enquiry into the Origin of Our Ideas of the Sublime and Beautiful* (1759), ed. J. T. Boulton (Notre Dame University Press, 1986).

7 Chambers, *Dissertation*, 36–37.

8 Fredrik Albritton Jonsson, "The Industrial Revolution in the Anthropocene," *Journal of Modern History* 84 (2012): 679–96.

9 Amy De'Ath, "Institutional Critique," in Imre Szeman & Dominic Boyer (eds), *Energy Humanities: An Anthology* (Johns Hopkins University Press, 2017), 23–25.

10 William Chambers, *Plans, Elevations, Sections, and Perspective Views of the Gardens and Buildings at Kew* (London, 1763), 2. See also Robin Middleton, "Chambers, W. 'A Treatise on Civil Architecture' London 1759," in John Harris & Michael Snodin (eds) *Sir William Chambers: Architect to George III* (Yale University Press, 1996), 68–76.

11 Magnus Olausson offers some evidence on this point in "Chambers and Sweden," Sir William Chambers, Harris & Snodin (eds), 11–18. On his Chinese "mask," see Chambers's own *Explanatory Discourse by Tan Chet-Qua, of Quang-Chew-Fu, Gent.* (1773; rpt. William Andrews Clark Memorial Library, 1978), 113.

12 Stanislaus Fung, "The Interdisciplinary Prospects of Reading Yuan Ye," *Studies in the History of Gardens and Designed Landscapes* 18, no. 3 (1998): 214, 219.

13 Cao Xueqin, *The Story of the Stone*, trans. David Hawkes (Penguin, 1973), Vol. 1 (*The Golden Days*), 334 and passim. The novel has also been known in English as *The Dream of the Red Chamber*. On Chambers's Western source material see Eileen Harris, "*Designs of Chinese Buildings and the Dissertation on Oriental Gardening*," in John Harris, *Sir William Chambers, Knight of the Polar Star* (A. Zwemmer, 1970), 144–62.

14 Olausson, "Chambers and Sweden," 11.

15 Dipesh Chakrabarty, "The Climate of History: Four Theses," *Critical Inquiry* 35 (2009): 197–222.

16 See, for example, the letter by Père d'Incarville published in the *Philosophical Transactions of the Royal Society of London* 48, no. 1 (1753): 253–60.

17 Buffon, *Epochs of Nature*, 59.

18 Chambers, *Explanatory Discourse*, 131.

19 Jack Flam (ed.) *Robert Smithson: The Collected Writings* (University of California Press, 1996), 152.

IN CONVERSATION WITH
JANINE RANDERSON

Janine Randerson is a New Zealand-based media artist and author whose work explores the intersection of art, technology, and science, especially as it pertains to weather and atmosphere. Much of her own work involves collaborations with meteorologists and climatologists, and her recent book *Weather as Medium: Toward a Meteorological Art* gathers together a wide range of artists who use weather as an aesthetic medium. Randerson spoke with **Karen M'Closkey + Keith VanDerSys** about the various ways artists are working with data and technology to engage the politics of science, climate, and community.

+ Tell us about your background and how you became interested in weather as a medium for art?

My background in interactive media—the fusing of different time-based mediums of sound, light, or video with sensing devices—led to an engagement with environmentally responsive work. Weather was a natural extension of my interest in landscape as a genre of experimental film-making. In 2006, I was invited to take part in a digital artist residency at the University of Waikato. During that time, I started attending meteorology courses and began working with micro-meteorologists who were measuring the carbon emissions from peat mining in Coromandel. I began sonifying that data as a way of exploring what patterns might emerge when the data is translated through another medium. So, I guess that was the moment where I started thinking seriously about meteorology and climate at the same time.

+ What work do you see as antecedents to your own work or the work of the many artists you discuss in your book *Weather as Medium: Toward a Meteorological Art*?

I start my (eccentric) history of weather with the deep time examples of the Garrwa people in Australia who, wearing white ochre, "co-perform" with the weather. Māori kites, Manu Tukutuku, are used to visualize wind currents partly for entertainment, for navigation, but sometimes flown at the death of an ancestor. If we look beyond western histories of painting and weather instruments and into indigenous cultures, there's also a long cultural history of performative sensory engagement with weather.

In terms of writers, Douglas Kahn's oeuvre, including his recent *Energies in the Arts*, was inspiring for his discussion of a natural history of media. Marshall McLuhan's *The Relation of Environment to Anti-Environment*, where he talks about media as the environmental envelope that we're wrapped in all the time was also important. Isabelle Stengers "Cosmopolitics" shaped my research, and her earlier work with Ilya Prigogine on chaos about the growing interest in ontogenesis, or how things emerge, in relation to a mediated environment.

Important forerunners who adopt weather as a live medium are Modernists such as Jean Dubuffet in the *Sols, Terre* series, where he worked with live rain-like sprays on lithographic stones, through to conceptual artists such as Phil Dadson on this side of the world, who made political works using wind to explode ink over his *Hoop Flags* (1970) to protest against a new motorway in Auckland. I'm always drawing on media historians who bring together the natural world with a variety of media, and the experiments of artists in creating fusions of weather and art media and social politics.

+ In your book, "medium" refers both to the weather itself, as well as to the other mediums by which we understand such temporal phenomena. When it comes to envisioning elusive things like pollution and climate change, we often hear the phrase "making the invisible visible," but making visible does not mean making "visual." Can you talk about non-visual mediums that you've worked with?

I often combine visual media with sound. I collaborated with urban meteorological scientist Jennifer Salmond who was monitoring CO_2 and NO_x along a busy main street in Auckland. In addition to data collection of these gases and temperature and humidity, we added sensors for Volatile Organic Compounds so we had an array of parameters to work with in the online artwork *Neighbourhood Air* (2012). With the help of computer scientists Jeff Nusz and Chris Manford that numerical data was interpreted into an abstract color field with sound. The air quality data was translated through different colors and sounds and then modified by inputs from an interactive sensory interface. I was also documenting people's impression of Auckland air quality through stories. Most people think that New Zealand is a very clean place but there are times when the air quality is quite poor and exceeded World Health Organization standards. The translation of the numerical data, through the stories of breathers of air and through sensory stimuli, really excited the urban meteorologist

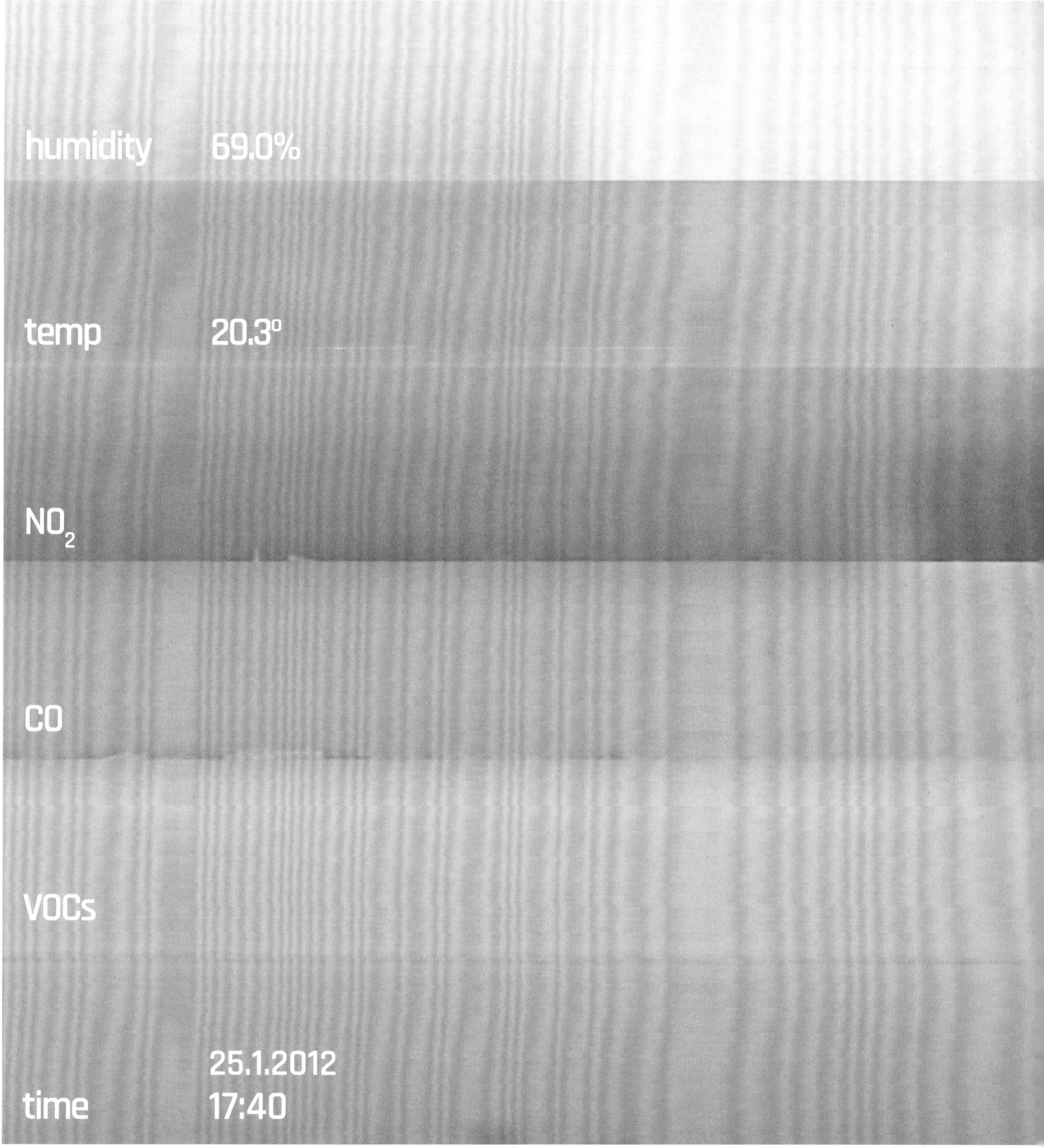

humidity   69.0%

temp   20.3°

NO_2

CO

VOCs

time   25.1.2012
17:40

Jennifer Salmond. We created an encounter with air quality information in a very different way to statistical analysis. We subsequently co-wrote an article for *Leonardo* and continue to collaborate.

+ So much of your work involves working with scientists. How important is it that artists know how to use the same instruments, data sets, or software that scientists use?

Artists tend to use the same instruments and data sets as scientists but in quite different ways. There's a chapter in *Weather as Medium* that looks at the work of Cameron Robbins, who takes a wind turbine and turns it into a drawing machine. Artists fashion surprisingly aberrant ways of working with instruments and data sets. Another example is raw data sets of satellite images given to me by Mike Wilmot from the Melbourne Bureau of Meteorology. Every hundred or so images, there was a sunlight flare in the image. This "flaw" would normally be removed from the data set. I was interested in exposing these moments to foreground the instrument's operation. This kind of improper use yielded possibilities or understandings that would normally remain hidden by standard scientific practices. Mike came to an exhibition where I was showing the translation of water vapor, infrared, and visible light data of the Japanese Meteorological satellite in the artwork the *Albedo of Clouds* (2011–2018). He was quite fascinated to see the information he works with every day represented differently.

+ Jennifer Gabrys, also interviewed in this issue of *LA+*, has worked on citizen-sensing projects about pollution. She notes that environments emerge from, and are not backdrop to, the use of such tools. You've said, "all software is a gathering" – is that a similar sentiment?

Yes, sensors actually create the environment rather than just detect it. I was interested in Gabrys's work while writing the book, and I was also thinking about these huge aggregated data sets. For example, in the *Most Blue Skies* (2006–2009) project, Joshua Portway and Lise Autogena were working with huge amounts of aggregated meteorological data to answer a simple question: where is the bluest sky in the world? Complex programming calculated the *most* blue place at any one moment and then they projected a small square of blue and a place name that would continuously change when exhibited in a gallery. They also sometimes collected social, qualitative data about the site selected by the calculations. On one particular day, the bluest sky site was in Australia, and the artists rang up and spoke to some of the townspeople about how they felt about the blueness of the sky that day. An important feature that I highlight in the book is that artists often use scientific datasets to express or expose their cultural meaning.

+ The artists that you highlight in your book seem to emphasize the social performance of data. Much of this type of work falls outside of the traditional fine-art context of institutional settings, like biennales and galleries. Do you think that's a unique feature of these types of practices?

Some artists in the book do work in traditional venues but I was trying to highlight the aspects of their work that involved social engagement. In Olafur Eliasson's well-known *Weather Project*, for example, he also interviewed gallery staff to gauge their perceptions and attitudes of weather. While I am interested in the perceptual effects of weather, it is equally important to try to situate or locate it in some way. My book chapter on "Social Meteorology and Participatory Art" was aimed at a kind of tribal polity in the case of Māori Artworks or Natalie Robertson's work. Even when her work was exhibited in a gallery, Māori elders performed a traditional ceremonial ritual, acknowledging the relationship to weather as ancestor, during the opening. So there's always a social-meteorological dimension in the work. I explore work that creates a community rather than an audience, which I think is an important distinction; work that pulls together communities into a shared pro-social ethos, working collectively, even if in a small way.

+ You've said that meteorological art keeps weather politics in circulation. Of course, we know that impacts from climate change are not evenly distributed. Are there enough artists tackling that side of the issue; that is, artists who are not just bringing the macro and micro together for an audience but highlighting the asymmetries of who is impacted?

I drew on indigenous, feminist, and colonial scholars to make that point in the book – particularly in relation to the work of Tongan artist Latai Taumoepeau. In "i-Land X-isle," Latai puts her body underneath a 500 kg melting ice block in a public space. She's really drawing attention to those who have been left out of that discourse, to say "here I am." It is a powerful work. It is often those who are most at risk from climate change, like small island nations, that are presented as victims and not given any sense of agency over what's happening. Latai's work is a means of reclaiming some of that agency.

+ You say that meteorological art sits in a philosophical tradition that displaces the human subject. In a project like Latai Taumoepeau's that you just mentioned, there is a form of bodily engagement that is often painful, which is very different from the notion of a more general "human subject." Can you speak about those differences in how you approach your work?

It's a matter of questioning our relentless subjectivity, or the idea of human exceptionalism, and to see ourselves as part of a broader eco-system. The body, therefore, becomes a feeling "receptor" of what is happening in the environment. That relates to the idea of weather media too, where information is not just formed in the delivery of weather *to* us, but also in the act of feeling or sensing the weather through our bodies. Karolina Sobecka's *Thinking like a Cloud* is a remarkable example. She asks people to drink the collected cloud vapors through agricultural meshes that collect the clouds. Clouds are full of microbiomes and other pollutants. So, by asking us to ingest the clouds, we tangibly feel the anthropogenic impacts of industrial activity in the body. We become a vehicle for experiencing the weather, just one part in a vast, complex system. So, I guess that's what I'm thinking about – displacing the human subject while at the same time calling attention to our bodies and our senses as something that's part of the environment.

+ You've remarked that the IPCC climate reports are the defining documents of our time. The scientists have already made the complicated models and data legible to us in the form of temperature limits and timeframes for action. If art's role is to raise awareness, how is that awareness different from other forms of consciousness-raising, whether in science or elsewhere?

There's a need to move past the task of raising awareness in artwork. That is no longer adequate because the issue isn't one of information scarcity. There's so much information out there – articles and reports, like the IPCC. The challenge for artists is to find engaging ways to communicate this information differently and to somehow permeate that malaise that stops us, even knowing all this, from actually acting on that information. So, I think that's the challenge for artists and scientists, activists, basically everybody who's concerned with making a difference is working out ways to inspire the collective.

While "inspire" may feel a bit hackneyed, Hannah Arendt's *Between Past and Future*–a key reference in my book–stresses the importance of inspiring principles as a theory of political action, which moves us to act beyond the self and instead act on behalf of the polity. Arendt says that we don't just live in a world that only scientists properly understand, and the rest of us only have a partial vision of what's really happening, but that we have to recognize other knowledge that cannot be captured by science. So artists are not mediators between "community knowledge" and "scientific knowledge" but also produce ways of seeing or knowing things. If art can show us Arendtian "inspiring principles" with actions that take place in the polis (public space), or allow us to understand some patterns of change through our bodies, it then complements and augments, and often challenges scientific activities.

+ Do you understand your work as a form of environmental activism?

Yes, I think so. On one level, the content of the work is a way of foregrounding and activating environmental issues politically on a public stage. So, it's very much akin to activism. But on the other hand, it's also about doing things that are other than activism; activism isn't necessarily focused on the sensory expansion of material understanding through the realm of affect and sensation. I am very interested in the aesthetic aspects of a work.

+ One last question, what project are you working on now?

I'm working with a research group in Australia around dark matter and scientific and artistic wonder. There's a physics lab (SUPL) in Stawell, in the Australian outback, which is soon to start using part of an old gold mine for sensing dark matter. There's a group of us at an early stage of thinking about how we can mediate between both the deep cultural histories of a 50,000-year-old culture in this area and the politics of big science and mining. The opportunity for dialogue around a project with a physics lab that is searching for this most mysterious of matter presents an exciting opening to explore how the community and science work together to understand something about dark matter and each other.

SHANNON MATTERN

GLIMMER:
REFRACTING ROCK

Shannon Mattern is professor of anthropology at The New School for Social Research. Her writing and teaching focus on media architectures and infrastructures and spatial epistemologies. She has written books about libraries, maps, and the history of urban intelligence, and she contributes a column to *Places Journal*. You can find her work at wordsinspace.net.

✚ MEDIA STUDIES, ANTHROPOLOGY, GEOLOGY

We're predisposed to perk up when we glimpse a glimmer in the Earth's crust. That shimmer might signal a coin fallen from someone's pocket into the dirt, a watering hole on a desert horizon, or gold or gemstones embedded in rock. We can even manufacture that geologic gleam by forming sidewalks from mica-infused concrete, or by spreading quartz-inflected stones as ground cover.

We've long sought to capture, to domesticate, to colonize that sparkle. If we were to walk into one of the many natural history museums that arose around the world in the 18th century, we'd likely encounter hundreds, if not thousands, of rocks and minerals, fastidiously arranged and labeled behind or beneath gleaming sheets of glass – the "very best of glass in the largest possible sizes," the Smithsonian's George Brown Goode recommended.[1] With such transparency, Brita Brenna explains, "the objects could be locked up, safe from dirt, dust and the touch of visitors, who could thus move around the museum without constant supervision."[2] Glass also allowed for maximum illumination. If a ray of sun caught a facet of feldspar just right, it might wink at us.

As museums later incorporated gas and electric lighting, curators sought to use these technologies to enhance their collections' visual appeal. Yet excessive light tended to damage materials, especially in art and ethnographic collections. And not all forms of artificial illumination were capable of capturing the full chromatic

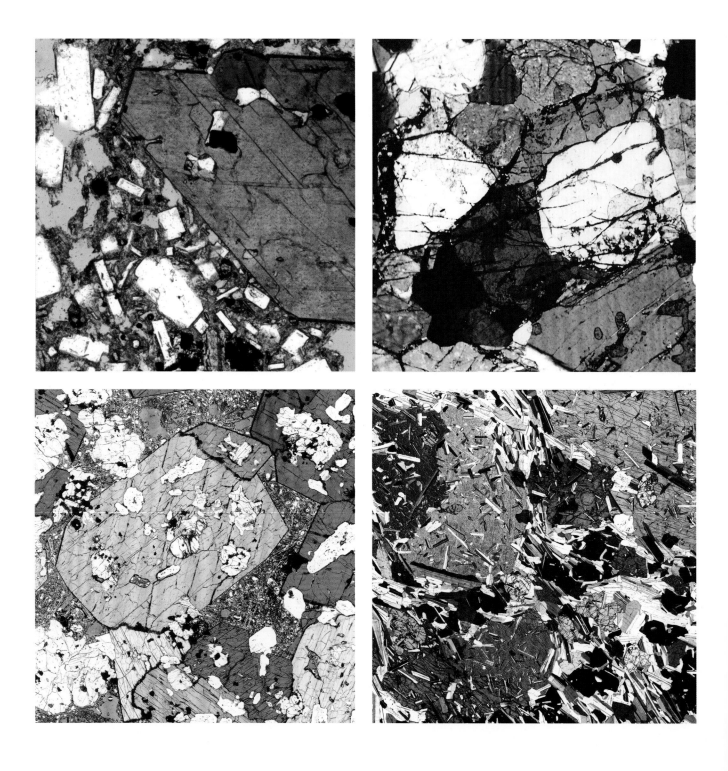

range of the objects on display. For instance, spectrally limited fluorescent lights, installed in some exhibition halls as early as the 1930s, tended to turn the mineral aquamarine, green – and to extinguish the star in star sapphires. The trend in the '60s, at least for art museums, was to transform the gallery into a "dark, mysterious cavern pierced by dramatic pin spotlights."[3] Chicago's Field Museum seemed to sustain this trend through the mid-'80s; in its renovated Grainger Hall of Gems, "slender beams [of light] from seemingly invisible sources reflected from jewel facets with laser-like intensity. Some gemstones rotated permanently on miniature carousels. The entire effect was dazzling."[4] With a bit of geologic stage design, these gems "appear[ed] to glow or sparkle with inner light."

Today, a curator might choose to use spotlighting, backlighting, neon, fiber-optic lighting, or LEDs. Anthropologist Corinne Kratz explains that exhibition lighting serves a range of functions: within the galleries, it defines paths and pacing, delineates zones, directs attention, and creates atmosphere; and when directed at exhibited objects, it focuses our gaze, highlights particular features and material properties, amplifies contrasts, and cultivates ambience or style.[5] In so doing, light—its quantity, intensity, color, distribution, form, and movement—serves a rhetorical purpose, making arguments or telling stories about the objects in its rays, or even inventing characters for them. White and natural light, for instance, tend to connote truth, realism, authenticity, and authority.[6] Concentrated boutique lighting, which appears to emerge from within the object, animates what it illuminates; a well-lit stone becomes vibrant matter.[7]

Light thus serves ontological and epistemological functions, too. It transforms rocks and minerals into knowledge objects – objects about which we can sense and know certain things, and (as we'll soon discover) objects that *themselves* know a great deal about us and our universe.[8] As Roger Caillois–himself an aggregate of many disciplinary ways of knowing–acknowledges, rocks "date from the beginnings of the planet, and perhaps emerged from another star."[9] Stones are cosmological and ontological repositories. And perhaps they refract a vision for the future, too. I'll propose that we can use experimental methods of illumination, particularly those that extend beyond our conventional humanly range of vision, to see stones as proxies for grappling with our long, craggy history of planetary disruption – and as mediators for our engagements with one another.

Even stones dull and mundane–those specimens Caillois describes as arousing no interest for the archaeologist, artist, collector, or diamond merchant; those that are "neither useful nor famous," that "do not sparkle in any ring"–yield their secrets through illumination.[10] With his own stone collection, some of which he cut into cross-sections and thin slices, illuminated, and photographed, Caillois looked not for "purity, brilliance, color, [and] structural rigor" – qualities a connoisseur would seek across all specimens of a type. Instead, Caillois sought the singularity of each object: the "curious alterations brought about

1 On glass: George Brown Goode, assistant secretary of the Smithsonian, *Annual Report, Board of Regents of the Smithsonian Institution, Showing the Operations, Expenditures, and Condition of the Institution for the Year Ending June 30, 1893* (Government Printing Office, 1895), 23. For more on the history of museums and the politics of display, particularly in natural history museums, see Tony Bennett, *The Birth of the Museum: History, Theory, Politics* (Routledge, 1995); Stephen T. Asma, *Stuffed Animals and Pickled Heads: The Culture and Evolution of Natural History Museums* (Oxford University Press, 2001); Carla Yanni, *Nature's Museums: Victorian Science and the Architecture of Display* (Princeton Architectural Press, 2005).

2 Brita Brenna, "Nature and Texts in Glass Cases," *Nordic Journal of Science and Technology Studies* 2, no. 1 (2014): 48. Ethnographic collections, and perhaps other kinds of institutions, once invited touch and other forms of multisensory engagement, according to Constance Classen and David Howes, "The Museum as Sensescape: Western Sensibilities and Indigenous Artifacts" in Elizabeth Edwards, Chris Gosden, & Ruth B. Phillips (eds), *Sensible Objects: Colonialism, Museums, and Material Culture* (Berg, 2006), 199–222. See also Tony Bennett, "Speaking to the Eyes: Museums, Legibility and the Social Order" in Sharon Macdonald (ed.), *The Politics of Display: Museums, Science, Culture* (Routledge, 2010), 22–30; Christopher Cuttle, *Light for Art's Sake: Lighting for Artworks and Museum Displays* (Routledge, 2013); and the work of ERCO, https://www.erco.com/en/.

3 Carol Kino, "It's Just Daylight, but It Has Endless Shades," *New York Times* (October 24, 2004), https://www.nytimes.com/2004/10/24/arts/design/its-just-daylight-but-it-has-endless-shades.html.

4 I changed all verbs to past tense. David M. Walsten & Edward Olsen, "A New Jewel in Field Museum's Crown: Grainger Hall of Gems Opens November 5," *Field Museum of Natural History Bulletin* 56, no. 10 (November 1985).

5 Corinne A. Kratz, "Rhetorics of Value: Constituting Worth and Meaning Through Cultural Display," *Visual Anthropology Review* 27, no. 1 (2011): 30, 32–33.

6 Ibid., 32.

Opposite (clockwise from top left): Photomicrographs of thin sections of andesite, bronzitite, gabbro, and gabbroic inclusions in andesite.

by the stone itself by means of metallic or other deposits, or...changes in shape due to erosion or serendipitous breakage."[11] Caillois, who fraternized with the surrealists and studied with the anthropologist Marcel Mauss, found various likenesses to landscapes in his rock sections, just as one finds forms in the clouds. He discerned in one particular slice of limestone the approximation of a human face, and he "meditated upon its furtive, shimmering lights and shades; on the interplay of parallels and obliques."[12]

Polarization

Archaeologist Christopher Tilley; anthropologists Penny Harvey, Tim Ingold, and Hugh Raffles; and medievalist Jeffrey Jerome Cohen likewise examine the idiosyncratic, dynamic qualities of rocks – how their "stoniness" varies in relation to their wetness or dryness, their position in light and shade.[13] Meanwhile, landscape architect Elise Hunchuck studies how stones mark boundaries and tell geological histories.[14] Geologists who study rocks, petrologists, also use light to extract information from geologic specimens.[15] A 30μm slice of rock–a thin section, not unlike those slices Caillois held in his collection–could be mounted on a glass slide and placed under a petrographic microscope. When the rock is positioned between the machine's two polarizing filters, light is transmitted through it, revealing particular properties–like crystal systems, cleavages, and color–that help to identify the rock's component minerals.

Sometimes the light source is intrinsic. Some mineral grains have the ability to absorb and store energy from environmental and cosmic radiation; when these "luminescent" grains are stimulated, they release their stored energy in the form of light – and this light offers clues to the specimens' geologic history. One luminescence dating method, optically-stimulated luminescence, measures the amount of radioactivity materials have accumulated "since the time they were buried."[16] Zircons, some of which are fluorescent, are formed through the crystallization of magma, are particularly durable, and are thus useful for dating rocks. As a rock weathers various geologic traumas, rings of zircon grow around the grain at its core; "like a tiny time capsule," Edmond Mathez explains, "the zircon records these events, each one of which may last hundreds of millions of years."[17]

In the lab, light transmitted through, reflected off, and emitting from materials serves as a means to date them, classify them, to piece together their biographies. Just as the light cast onto the museum's display cases transformed their enclosed specimens into objects to be interpreted by museum visitors, here, these optical laboratory methods permit geoscientists to extract data from their subjects. As the instructors of an Open University "Introduction to Petrology" class tell their students, "Rocks are the history books of the planet. Meteorite impacts, collisions and rifting of ancient continents, erosion of long vanished mountain ranges, ice ages, and life itself have all left records in these books." We just have to learn how to crack their "complex code."[18]

Shine

It's quite a cryptographic conundrum. Caillois was taken by those stones that defied decryption and classification. Art historian Donna Roberts describes how he delighted in casting light on stones' ambiguities, their "seeming at once animate and inanimate, organic and inorganic, mineral and vegetal, useful and useless, the stuff of poetic reverie and cultural symbolism as well as raw material."[19] We are fascinated by stones, he claimed, because of their severity, their radiance, their impenetrability, and their intransigence.[20] Caillois focused on those that mean nothing to architecture, sculpture, mosaic, jewelry; they shone for no one but themselves. His chosen rocks "only attest to their own presence."

But this is true of hardly any stone – especially not those in a museum vitrine or a laboratory. We illuminate and irradiate them in order to extract and collect and classify them; and they, in turn, reflect light back on us. Their luminescence backlights our histories of colonialism, which as countless historians have noted, constitute the bedrock of the natural sciences, cultures of collection, and the institutions we created to study and store their spoils. Geographer Kathryn Yusoff argues that "geologic classification enabled the transformation of territory into a readable map of resources and organized the apprehension of extraction and the designation of extractable territories...The motivation of colonialism was an extraction project."[21] And it then transformed those extracted materials into radiant cathedrals in the new colonial cities, and opulent palaces and crown jewels back at home.

Even the gleam of today's mica-inflected landscaping stones, granite countertops, tombstones, and marble tiles is refracted through expansive geopolitics.[22] More than half of all of the United States' "dimension stone"–natural rock or stone that has been selected and cut to specific dimensions–is likely imported, primarily from China, India, and Brazil, or it is harvested in the US and processed abroad. Poor information about stone's supply chain, and the labor conditions and environmental impacts along it, make it very difficult to reckon with the costs and consequences of all that lithic gleam.[23]

We might think, too, about the oppressively visceral shine at many sites of extraction, where miners toil in unregulated pits under a relentless glare, struggling to discern the glimmer of gold or gem through sun-blinded eyes. Eco-literacy scholar Rebecca Griggs tells of iridescent indices on the Australian landscape – portents for prospectors, lighting the way to a lode:

> Folklore has it that fossickers and small-claims prospectors once believed the Pilbara's buried metals could be read upside down in the sky. They'd scan incoming storms for 'lightning nests' – electrical clusters towed around the low-hanging cloud cover by the polarity of minerals below ground. Where lightning lingered, or struck the ground repetitively, a lode was thought to lie folded between sedimentary layers.[24]

In order to acknowledge the cultural and political-economic histories of stone, rather than reading upside down, maybe we need to illuminate from below, to find the elemental sources of superficial shine, to light with the dark. Black feminist and critical race theorists, attuned to the politics of light(ness) and (in)visibility, offer us several productively unsettling and ultimately reparative ways of seeing. Art historian Krista Thompson, in her study of African diasporic aesthetic practice, focuses on the visual economy of "shine": the prominence of mirrors and starbursts in street photographs, the glitz of dancehalls, the radiant pageantry of proms, the bling of hip-hop videos. Rather than signaling superficial materialism, she proposes, these cultural forms and modes of illumination represent "everyday aspirational practices of black communities, who make and do more with what they have, creating prestige through the resources at hand."[25] What's radical and critical about these consumptive practices is that they "disrupt notions of value" by elevating shine, which emanates *from* the commodity object, over the object itself.

Perhaps rather than regarding shine as a superficial external effect of a more corporeally integral radiance, we need to learn to read shine itself as meaningful – and especially so to particular communities that have historically been excluded from capitalist commodity networks, or have borne the injustices of capitalism's and colonialism's extractive demands. This re-reading constitutes a new methodology, one that's more attentive to the racialized (and classed and gendered) cultural politics of visuality. Thompson offers bling as a "black popular and scholarly approach that is attentive to diasporic people's intrinsic place within, estrangement from, or relationship to modern capitalism."[26]

Blacklight

How do we recalibrate our eyes to bring shine itself into relief – to transform glimmer into a *figure* on a white supremacist and colonialist *ground*? Critical race scholar

7 Jane Bennett, *Vibrant Matter: A Political Ecology of Things* (Duke University Press, 2010).

8 I am grateful to @AAPiccini, @AlJavieera, @annelysegelman, @asfaltics, @bamendelsohn, @blprnt, @dietoff, @figuralities, @GoldsmithLeo, @guykeulemans, @hulknet, @infopetal, @KeysWalletPh0ne, @lifewinning, @mfkomie, @schettinodesign, @sirosenbaum, @siteations, @tamars, @ThandiLoewenson, @UbuLoca, @wileycount, and @yeslev for sharing relevant resources for this project via Twitter.

9 Roger Caillois, "Stones & Other Texts, an excerpt," trans Válentine Umansky, *Sensate* 1+2 (2018), http://sensatejournal.com/stones-other-texts/.

10 Roger Caillois, "Extracts from Stones," trans. Jean Burrell, *Diogenes* 207 (2005): 89.

11 Roger Caillois, *The Writing of Stones*, trans. Barbara Bray (University Press of Virginia, 1970), 4, 6.

12 Ibid., 103.

13 Jeffrey Jerome Cohen, *Stone: An Ecology of the Human* (University of Minnesota Press, 2015); Penny Harvey, "Lithic Vitality: Human Entanglement with Nonorganic Matter," in Penny Harvey, Christian Krohn-Hansen, & Knut G. Nustad (eds), *Anthropos and the Material* (Duke University Press, 2019), 143–60; Tim Ingold, "Materials Against Materiality," *Archaeological Dialogues* 14, no. 1 (2007): 1–16; Hugh Raffles, "A Lapidary Itinerary," *Rocks Stones Dust* (n.d.), http://rocksstonesdust.com/essays/raffles.html; Hugh Raffles, "Twenty-Five Years is a Long Time," *Cultural Anthropology* 27, no. 4 (August 2012): 526–34; Christopher Tilley, *The Materiality of Stone: Explorations in Landscape Phenomenology* (Berg, 2004).

14 Elise Hunchuck, excerpts from *Tsunami Stones* (2017), https://cargocollective.com/elisehunchuck/An-Incomplete-Atlas-of-Stones-1.

15 Much of the following discussion is drawn from the following sources: Jing Niu, "Introduction to Optical Mineralogy" (October 21, 2012), https://www.youtube.com/watch?v=_ooSuUHGiiw; "Optical Properties of Minerals," *GeologyScience*, http://geologyscience.com/general-geology/optical-properties-of-minerals/; "Other Dating Techniques," *Earth Science Australia*, http://earthsci.org/space/space/geotime/otherdatingtechniques/otherdatingtechniques.html; Daniel J. Peppe, "Dating Rocks and Fossils Using Geologic Methods," *Nature* (2013), https://www.nature.com/scitable/knowledge/library/dating-rocks-and-fossils-using-geologic-methods-107924044; Peter W. Reiners, et al., *Geochronology and Thermochemistry* (Wiley, 2018); University of New England, Geology 209, "Properties of Minerals in Thin Section" (March 2, 2018), https://www.youtube.com/watch?v=4WWAyYSVogU.

16 Peppe, "Dating Rocks and Fossils Using Geologic Methods," ibid.

17 Edmond A. Mathez, "Zircon Chronology: Dating the Oldest Material on Earth," American Museum of Natural History, https://www.amnh.org/learn-teach/curriculum-collections/earth-inside-and-out/.

Denise Ferreira da Silva proposes that blacklight, or ultraviolet radiation—which is what irradiates many dance floors and makes fluorescent rocks glow in the dark—can "turn opaque things into luminous ones."[27] It then "works *through* that which makes it shine," and transforms its medium in the process.[28] UV light, in working through the body, prompts it to produce vitamin D, and it's been used to treat skin conditions like psoriasis, eczema, and scleroderma. But it can also cause sunburn and skin cancer, accelerate skin aging, and damage DNA. While UV is beyond the spectrum of human vision, it can harm the eyes by damaging the retina, burning the cornea, and causing cataracts and macular degeneration. What we can't see can hurt us – and potentially exacerbate our blindness.

This is an all-too-convenient metaphor for whiteness, colonialism, and other systems of oppression that undergirded the rise of the natural history museum and, as Yusoff notes, geology itself. All those deleterious and carcinogenic properties of UV, Silva argues, ultimately serve to productively decompose, to "break the code" of, our malignantly colonialist and racist systems of classification and valuation.

Recalibrating our eyes for shine and blacklight—repositioning figure and ground; looking beyond our naturalized spectrum of vision, beyond the "color line," as W.E.B. Du Bois conceived it—requires accepting both the constructive and deconstructive, the comfortable and uncomfortable aspects of prying open sore eyes. It compels us to recognize that colonial and racial violence structure the very "analytical tools" we use to think about global capital, and that "colonial violence remains active in the global present."[29] Blacklight, "a black feminist reading device," Silva says, "focuses on the elusive, the unclear, the uncertain," perhaps not unlike Caillois's illumination of "paradoxes of classification, ontological slippages and confusions that reveal the limitations for knowledge in strictly separating the poetic from the scientific."[30] Even the geochemistry of fluorescence itself is somewhat of a mystery to petrologists.[31]

But there is more at stake for Silva, because she's not merely drawing playfully "inadmissible similarities," as Caillois was, between rock sections and landscapes and human portraits.[32] She's blacklighting colonialist legacies of classification wherein a black body is coded differently, lesser, than a white one; where an enslaved or incarcerated black body extracts the bling that then adorns and enriches the white body. Silva's blacklight aims to work *through* the typical occlusion of racial and colonial violence—a craggy, opaque, long-buried rock that would really rather reflect than transmit those revelatory rays—and makes it fluoresce. Her blacklight "prepares the ground," she says, "for an imaging of the world and its existents in which reflection gives into the imagination."[33]

Perhaps that imaging requires that we look beyond the vitrines and microscopes, the specimen labels and thin sections, to the colonial context of geology and the settler-colonial provenance of its objects. Combining Thompson's and Silva's methods,

18 "An Introduction to Minerals and Rocks under the Microscope," "Introduction to Petrology," Geological Sciences, Open University (Spring 1999), https://www.open.edu/openlearn/ocw/mod/oucontent/view.php?id=9265&printable=1.

19 Donna Roberts, "An Introduction to Caillois' Stones & Other Texts," *Flint* 1/2 (2018); reprinted, http://sensatejournal.com/an-introduction-to-caillois-stones-other-texts/. For more on unclassifiable rocks, see Sophia Roosth, "Come and Forget the Organism," Canadian Centre for Architecture (January 24, 2019), https://www.cca.qc.ca/en/events/63037/.

20 Roger Caillois, "Stones & Other Texts, an excerpt," ibid.

21 Kathryn Yusoff, *A Billion Black Anthropocenes or None* (University of Minnesota Press, 2018), 83. See also Maria Margaret Lopes & Irina Podgorny, "The Shaping of Latin American Museums of Natural History, 1850–1990," *Osiris* 15 (2000): 110.

22 Although it is possible to conceive of stone construction that is embedded in its particular place of origin. Harvey describes contemporary Andean inhabitants who are "still very attentive to the vitality of stone in ways that demonstrate continuities with Inka understandings of material vitality. Many large rocks are thought to channel the energetic life-giving forces of the earth." Harvey, 153.

23 Meg Calkins, "Solid as a Rock," *Landscape Architecture Magazine* (February 27, 2018).

24 Rebecca Giggs, "Open Ground," *Griffith Review* 47 (2015).

25 Krista Thompson, *Shine: The Visual Economy of Light in African Diasporic Aesthetic Practice* (Duke University Press, 2015): 25. *E-flux* has also taken up "shine" in two issues: *e-flux* 61 (January 2015), https://www.e-flux.com/journal/61/; and "Politics of Shine," *e-flux Supercommunity* (2015), http://supercommunity.e-flux.com/topics/politics-of-shine/.

26 Thompson, *Shine*, 26.

27 Denise Ferreira da Silva, "Blacklight" in Clare Molloy & Philippe Pirotte (eds), *Otobong Nkanga: Luster and Lucre* (Sternberg Press, 2017), 245.

28 Denise Ferreira da Silva, "In the Raw," *e-flux* 93 (September 2018), https://www.e-flux.com/journal/93/.

Opposite: Installation views of "In Pursuit of Bling" (2014) by Otobong Nkanga.

Nigerian-born, Belgium-based artist Otobong Nkanga, in her *In Pursuit of Bling* installation-performance, deconstructs the traditional vitrine to display mica and other materials that, as Silva says, "glitter-image colonial violence."[34] On an assemblage of low-lying tables of variable heights, Nkanga arranges "raw" ore and mineral samples; examples of the products and artifacts, like cosmetics and ornaments, that these minerals generate; diagrams of their crystalline structure; and archival materials documenting their excavation.[35] Nkanga explains that "by examining what mica looks like in its chemical structure, looking at the component elements that are in it"—thus adopting the optical methods of the lab—"I thought that maybe it's interesting to put all these ideas together within a structure connected by magnetic rods, with which you can change the display or let's say the molecular structure of the exhibition, adjusting each table to different exhibitions."[36] The overhead lighting casts a gridded shadow on the floor, transforming the entire installation into a topographic terrain.

At the center of each array is a tapestry. One features a gemstone abstracted as a diagram with exaggeratedly denoted "bling." The stone floats atop a relief map that alludes to the geographic terrain from which the material is extracted, but which is labeled not with landforms, but with the minerals' chemical elements and compounds – from Barium to Zinc. The other tapestry features two bodies, a man and a woman, whose upper halves are replaced with tiered platforms that allude simultaneously to the lab table, the exhibition vitrine, and the landscape of extraction. These figures' tiered torsos and heads mirror the architecture of the installation itself – or perhaps they *refract* it, bringing all the molecular modeling, mining, and manufacturing to bear, both physically and metaphorically, on the bodies that perform the precarious labor of "turning opaque things into luminous ones." And by situating those bodies within larger topologies and topographies, Nkanga traces the supply chain connecting "spaces of shine" to "places of obscurity" – and thereby "illuminat[es] that which must remain obscure for the fantasy of freedom and equality to remain intact."[37]

This de-obfuscation ultimately allows for a "[re-]imaging of the world." What we might also see refracted in Nkanga's multi-scalar diagram of "bling" is what Yusoff describes as "the imagination of a hundred million Anthropocenes that adequately map the differentiated power geometries of geology and its uneven mobilization through different geosocial formations."[38] By blacklighting the Anthropocene—that geological age distinguished by the dominance of human influence, effected by mining and industrial manufacturing—we painfully "draw attention to the violence [and racism] at its core," but we also open ourselves up to the validation and adoption of other more liberatory, reparative ways of seeing and knowing, and, ideally, more responsible ways of *being*.[39] Heather Davis and Zoe Todd call for "the consideration of Indigenous philosophies and processes of Indigenous self-governance as a necessary political corrective, alongside the self-determination of other communities and societies violently impacted by the white

29 Silva, "Blacklight," 245; "1 (life) ÷ 0 (blackness) = ∞ − ∞ or ∞ / ∞; On Matter Beyond the Equation of Value," *e-flux* 79 (February 2017), https://www.e-flux.com/journal/79/.

30 Silva, "Blacklight," 250; Roberts, "An Introduction to Caillois' Stones."

31 "Essentially, ultraviolet light shining on these minerals is absorbed into the rock, where it reacts with chemicals in the material and excites the electrons in the mineral, thus emitting that energy as an outwardly glow. Different types of ultraviolet light—longwave and shortwave—can produce different colors from the same rock, and some rocks that have other materials inside them (called activators) may glow multiple colors." Jennifer Billock, "Follow This Rainbow Tunnel to the World's Largest Collection of Fluorescent Rocks," *Smithsonian* (March 28, 2017), https://www.smithsonianmag.com/travel/largest-collection-fluorescent-rocks-180962572/.

32 Caillois, "Diagonal Science" in Claudine Frank (ed.), *The Edge of Surrealism: A Roger Caillois Reader* (Duke University Press, 2003), 355.

33 Silva, "Blacklight," 252.

34 Silva, "1 (life)..."

35 Philippe Pirotte, "Foreword" in Clare Molloy & Philippe Pirotte (eds), *Otobong Nkanga: Luster and Lucre* (Sternberg Press, 2017), 9.

36 Otobong, Nkanga, Clare Molloy & Fabian Schöneich, "Intricate Connections" in ibid., 174.

37 Silva, "1 (life)..."

38 Kathryn Yusoff, "Epochal Aesthetics: Affectual Infrastructures of the Anthropocene," *e-flux* (March 29, 2017), https://www.e-flux.com/architecture/accumulation/121847/.

39 Heather Davis & Zoe Todd, "On the Importance of a Data, or Decolonizing the Anthropocene," *ACME: An International Journal for Critical Geographies* 16, no. 4 (2017): 763.

40 Consider the indigenous museology of The Natural History Museum, a traveling exhibit advised by a team of indigenous representatives; or the feminist-indigenous science advocated for and practiced by Kim Tall Bear and Max Liboiron see Indigenous STS (http://indigenoussts.com/) and the Civic Laboratory for Environmental Action Research (https://civiclaboratory.nl/).

41 Katherine McKittrick, "Rift," in Antipode Editorial Collective (ed), *Keywords in Radical Geography: Antipode at 50* (Hoboken, NJ: Wiley Blackwell, 2019): 246. McKittrick does not explicitly mention the life sciences, but I think it's important to entangle them, too, since our geologic pasts and futures do not belong solely to the human. See also Lauret Savoy: *Trace: Memory, History, Race, and the American Landscape* (Counterpoint, 2016).

supremacist, colonial, and capitalist logics instantiated in the origins of the Anthropocene." How might we refract Indigenous, black, and feminist Anthropocenes—and a hundred million more—through the rocks in our labs and landscapes and vitrines, through the ways we do science, shape the earth, and construct "natural" history?[40]

We have cast light upon rocks in order to crack their geochemical code – to read them as cosmological repositories, time capsules, history books, material missives from distant stars. Yet rocks don't only record the past; if lit just right, their glow can illuminate a pathway toward the future. Cultural geographer Katherine McKittrick reminds us that the natural sciences, life sciences, cultural history, and affect are "knotted knowledge systems that can read our planetary futures outside market time."[41] Rocks, among the most prosaic of objects, lend themselves to observation through these various lenses largely because of their seeming simplicity and resilience. Perhaps they're the ideal prisms, or lithic lanterns, through which we can backlight an overdetermined past and shine forward into a hundred million possible futures.

IMAGE CREDITS

The Rocks Must Be Strange

p. 94–95: "Artificial volcano eruption on the man-made rock island Stein" (2011) by H.U. Küenle, used under CC BY SA 3.0 license.

p. 96: "The Stone of Wörlitz" (1979) aquatint by Wilhelm Friedrich Schlotterbeck after Carl Kuntz, used with permission via Kulturstiftung Dessau-Wörlitz.

p. 98: "A View of the Wilderness at Kew" aquatint (1763) by William Marlow, public domain via The Metropolitan Museum of Art, by Harris Brisbane Dick Fund, 1925.

In Conversation with Janine Randerson

p. 100–101: Image by Yutong Zhan, incorporating "Cloud Study (Distant Storm)" (c. 1786–1806) by Simon Denis, public domain via The Whitney Collection, Gift of Wheelock Whitney III, and Purchase, Gift of Mr. and Mrs. Charles S. McVeigh, by exchange, 2003.

p. 103: "Neighbourhood Air" (2011) by Janine Randerson, used with permission.

Glimmer: Refracting Rock

p. 106: "Gold" (2007) by Simon Law, used under CC BY SA 2.0 license.

p. 108: "Rock Thin Section Andesite" (2009) by Cheryl Cameron, public domain via US Geological Survey; "Bronzitite" (2005) by Kevin Walsh, used under CC BY 2.0 license; "Gabbro from Rum in Scotland" (2012) by Julien Leuthold, used under CC BY 3.0 license; "Photomicrograph of Rock Thin Section Gabbroic Inclusion" (2018) by public domain via US Geological Survey.

p. 113: "In Pursuit of Bling – The Discovery" and "In Pursuit of Bling – The Transformation" (2014) by Otobong Nkanga, installation photographs by Anders Sune Berg, used with permission. These works by Otobong Nkanga were exhibited at the 8th Berlin Biennale for Contemporary Art, KW Institute for Contemporary Art, May 29–August 3, 2014.

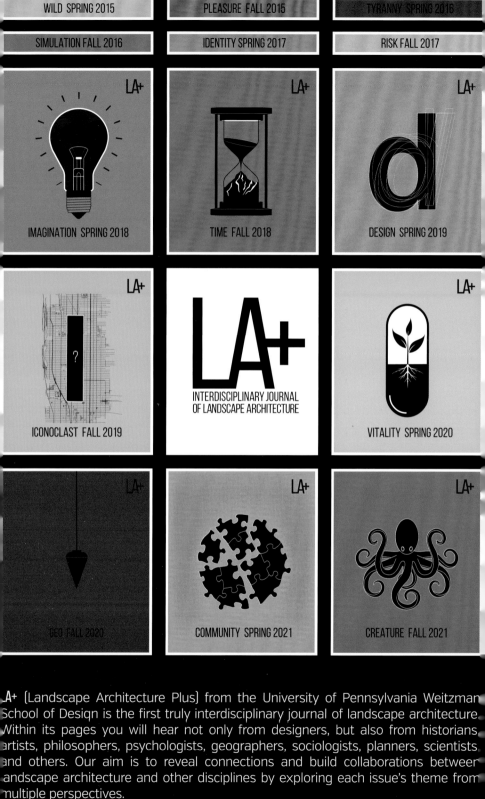

LA+ (Landscape Architecture Plus) from the University of Pennsylvania Weitzman School of Design is the first truly interdisciplinary journal of landscape architecture. Within its pages you will hear not only from designers, but also from historians, artists, philosophers, psychologists, geographers, sociologists, planners, scientists, and others. Our aim is to reveal connections and build collaborations between landscape architecture and other disciplines by exploring each issue's theme from multiple perspectives.

LA+ brings you a rich collection of contemporary thinkers and designers in two issues each year. To subscribe follow the links at WWW.LAPLUSJOURNAL.COM